# Soundtrack for the Dead

John Reed

Soundtrack for the Dead

Olympia Publishers
*London*

www.olympiapublishers.com
OLYMPIA PAPERBACK EDITION

Copyright © John Reed 2024

The right of John Reed to be identified as author of
this work has been asserted in accordance with sections 77 and 78 of
the Copyright, Designs and Patents Act 1988.

**All Rights Reserved**

No reproduction, copy or transmission of this publication
may be made without written permission.
No paragraph of this publication may be reproduced,
copied or transmitted save with the written permission of the publisher,
or in accordance with the provisions
of the Copyright Act 1956 (as amended).

Any person who commits any unauthorised act in relation to
this publication may be liable to criminal
prosecution and civil claims for damage.

A CIP catalogue record for this title is
available from the British Library.

ISBN: 978-1-80439-604-9

This is a work of fiction.
Names, characters, places and incidents originate from the writer's
imagination. Any resemblance to actual persons, living or dead, is
purely coincidental.

First Published in 2024w

**Olympia Publishers**
**Tallis House**
**2 Tallis Street**
**London**
**EC4Y 0AB**

Printed in Great Britain

# INTRO

The sky is different here: European, Mediterranian blue. Some kind of blue you don't see in New York City.

The sea is different. I don't know why.

I live in Italy now. And I'll stay here forever. Literally. I'm dying. Cancer, no chance to survive, but that's OK – I'll try to explain the paradox.

(It is not really a paradox, it's just a possibility of consciousness.)

I should be careful now, very careful. I may not fuck up this time.

I should be careful with sentences, with words: not many are necessary. I must be clear, deadly clear. Probably subject + predicate + object should do just fine. Ellipsis even.

I have to eliminate time if there is no more time. I should eliminate verb tenses if possible.

There are only a few words needed to die properly. I'll try to find them.

Words are trivial.

## SONIC YOUTH: PROTECT ME YOU

My body is falling apart. My country is sinking into chaos. No one can save me nor the United States of America. No medicine, no constitutional amendment. This ain't a pessimistic prophecy. It's a logical absurd. God invented it.

I left New york. I still have time enough to tell a story. It should be a joke, I suppose. A killing joke. I'm already laughing: I need another dose of painkillers to proceed. It's not morphine yet – the funniest substance comes only at the very end.

(In my case: six months, maybe more, but definetely less than a year.)

I will use irony, nothing else. Without proof I find it as the only useful method against fear.

Irony, of course, includes God. God is a joke too. Actually, he invented irony before all the rest was completed.

(You doubt? – Check the Old Testament. Choose any passage. My hint: Deuteronomy 25: 11-12)

My decision to travel by ship to Europe was simple: it wasn't necessary; it was hopeless, therefore ironic; I wasn't in a hurry. Besides, I hate planes.

So I set sail from New York to Italy.

(Also a plane could crash. This would be in my case – it goes without saying – absolutely unacceptable. I cannot die in a fucking plane crash just because Boeing was making a huge profit with some cheaper components. With all due respect to irony, I'm leaving this lucky opportunity to fat, rich, pale purple tourists on their way to Paris.)

I chose a ship. I wanted to really feel the ocean before I sunk into it. In the middle of Atlantic the feeling was good. Beyond fear. The people on board were frightened as they watched the endless surface of the ocean. They were waiting for the paradise on the other side. Nothing happened. Eternity was there, waiting exclusively for me.

Nobody will miss me. Nobody will even notice that I'm gone. Just like Kafka's »*Hunger Artist*«. In the »good ol' days« (the most desgusting phrase in the world, totaly ironicless) people were employed. Evidence was important. Absence from work was almost a crime. People were wanted. But not in the twenty-first century. Your contract ain't worth a shit. You can be replaced in a second. You're an IT mastermind? – So is chimpanzee or at least some Shramipamivami guy from India. Your contribution ain't worth a shit. Anyone can do it. And at the end of time, artificial intelligence will do it all. And it will happen soon – the end of time, of course.

You can disappear any time. The landlord may be pissed for a while, if you didn't pay the rent.

Feed the neighbor's cat if you can, and leave.

I bought a ship ticket to the other side with Hunter S. Thompson's sentences in my mind:

»*We are all alone, born alone, die alone, and – in spite of True Romance magazines – we shall all someday look back on our lives and see that, in spite of our company, we were alone the whole way. I do not say lonely – at least, not all the time – but essentially, and finally, alone.*«

I was alone before. In New York City. Everywhere. It was a privilege, I fought for it. There is a basic distinction between

»being alone« and »being lonely«. Being alone is a state of mind, even a state of power. Loneliness – on the contrary – means you forgot to shoot yourself. Loneliness equals pathetic.

(Living in Antarctica could be used as an excuse, but still ... there are emperor penguins all around you.)

I was alone in a relationship. We all are. Especially married couples. In the West, relationships are no longer possible. At some point, everyone wants to kill their partner and buy a much more sexy television set instead. I realized that for good when my ex-girlfriend once brought home some unusual South American plants, species that are supposed to be the main source of curare.

(I became suspicious because she never grew plants. She loved steel and concrete. She should have killed me with a hammer, not using poison.)

Atlantic Ocean was... not. It was nothing. One big fucking nothing. You're aware of it, but you cannot describe it. I wanted to believe – this is death! This is what it looks like! I don't want any surprises, especially not the afterlife. If I die, I die. Everything disappears and the invisible ocean is beautiful.

(But the fear remains. It won't go away. We are permanently aware of fear. And we are left alone with it.)

I should describe the route with ship. I should mention whales. I should have done it like the realist authors of the nineteenth century, the famous novelists.

I cannot, it's impossible. In the twenty-first century, no one expects written details. We use images. Sounds and images. We watch, we don't read. I have to be fast. I have to use fraud and fear.

This is my only option. Most likely, I am going to fail. My only hidden ace up my sleeve is fear.

(This is a risky bet. But it often wins because fear ain't my private property. We all share it. I use it as a very seductive bait.)

After about a week we sailed past the Azores.

For a moment, just for a moment, I forgot about my dying. I watched these people. The future is theirs. They own it. Flat-Earthers from all around the globe. Not just from the Bible Belt. Retirees who control global finances with their funds. The last surviving retirees. After the neoliberal revolution is finished, there will no longer be a single retiree in this world any more.

(And probably the world will no longer be.)

Americans, mostly. Some old fat fucks in Hawaiian shirts; their wannabe Dolly Parton wives; grotesque youngsters, grandchildren, eating ice cream, screaming I scream. An insult to evolution. Small American paper flags. Noise pollution, visual pollution. Pollution. Future.

Our journey should take about fourteen days with five stops enroute. On the eleventh day we entered Gibraltar. The excitement grew. Europe above on the left, Africa below on the right. The Old World. A controversial definition. »The New World« is aging faster than anyone expected. Maybe »The Old World« could become younger soon. Without plastic surgery.

I have always had ambivalent feelings about Europe. I am an American by conviction. But I like Europe. European sophistication in thinking and emotions. Why could The Rolling Stones understand and accept our culture as an ideal while we denied it? We didn't even want to know it exists. Because it was black, for example. Why did Europe admire Edgar Allan Poe long before we did?

Are we really so vulgar? Or just too religious to acknowledge any kind of blasphemy, any law besides the Old

Testament. Forgiveness was never our quality. Our Nazarene is a rasist who never forgives. A prophet with a shotgun. We punish. Our God is a very old God of vengeance. Our GOOD means one, our EVIL means zero. There is nothing inbetween. It's no surprise that the digital revolution has begun in the USA. I'm white American. I'm forty-nine years old. I'm a slender figure. No additional information about a person is essential.

(I am »slender« now. In a few months I will look like an example of PR materials for Auschwitz.)

My God is on permanent vacation. We meet from time to time to discuss the quality of coffee from Honduras or the one from Uganda. He laughs always and says: »*Did you know, my dear friend, all the primitives in the world call it Arabica. People never understood my basic idea. They never will.*«

(He never takes cream or sugar. I wonder why not. He is not really afraid of diabetes, I suppose. Or... maybe I just don't understand his basic idea.)

Entering the Mediterranian can in no way be compared to the ocean. The soul breathes here, but dies there. Too many stories are hidden here behind every stone, death is temporary, sitting in a waiting room.

Spain, France, Italy: I enter Catholic lands now. Should I listen to Gregorian chants?

(They did fit into the ocean, I admit that.)

What's the song for the dead?
- Medieval mysticism. (No such thing in the USA.)
- A prayer. (Boring. Waste of time.)
- Warrior scream. (Misunderstanding.)
- Hymn. (Lobotomized only.)
- Classical music. (Isn't it immortal?)

Rock'n'roll? – The only genre that combines both: sex and

death. The only two essences that equally describe the only one secret about our lives. It is no surprise, we almost die in orgasm: it's so close to death. This is the main natural symbiosis.

Rock'n'roll is the most underestimated, underrated genre. It's not a coincidence, all the cultures (American especially) in the world (without any exception) were (and are) so afraid of it: because it was always telling the truth. The truth about our passions and fears.

Rock'n'roll is the most influential political agenda of all times. And it sounds good.

So let it be rock'n'roll.

(Though I admire Gregorian chants just as much.)

Adriatic Sea. Last route. Coast, islands everywhere. Suddenly the fear returned, it came back with devastating power. I continued reading, fast, as if in panic, screaming for help. Hunter S. Thompson reminded me again painfully:

»*I understand that fear is my friend, but not always. Never turn your back on fear. It should always be in front of you, like a thing that might have to be killed.*«

I have always admired this guy. He had an amazing ability to combine the intimate and the social, gun and pussy, with an equally sharp emphasis on both. He understood that intimacy is always political at the same time. A pretty fucked up finding – the same as Freud's actually, only with more loaded guns.

Port of Trieste, Italy. End of the road.

Retirees were ready to divide and conquer. Last American conquistadors. Last valid credit cards.

(Meanwhile, enormously rich were on their ships too: spaceships. Escape into the universe. All the rats are running away.)

I left the ship. Standing on the pier I had two options:

commit suicide or take medication. I heard my heart beating on the verge of serious tachycardia or an unbearable anxiety attack. My desperation grew, I felt pins and needles in my legs, in my arms. I could barely breathe, some white light was blinding me, the veins in my neck felt like thunder.

I ate the pills quickly. Many pills. Too many. It didn't matter.

(Honestly: there were a lot of various opioids among them. The best thing about American health insurance – if you can afford it – is your doctor doesn't prescribe medicine, you order medicine. If you pay for it, you get it. This is how our medical competition works. So I got all the opioids in this world without any problems, plus exstra prescriptions. And without fear of the authorities, neither in the USA nor in Europe.)

I sat down on the suitcase. Passengers and tourists were leaving the pier.

My only luggage was a cardboard suitcase, very old but well preserved. I inherited it from my father. To whom it belonged, was a basement mystery. Red and yellow, probably fancy in times past. Maybe it was an Old-World-suitcase on an unexpected way back home.

I had a lot of books inside and almost no wardrobe. The plan was simple: if I live (as long as) I buy my next pants or underpants or what-fucking-ever-needed in Italy. They do have some designers these Italians, right? All those shitheads back on Wall Street would kill for Armani and Versace.

(Fuck Armani! – If I need socks, Italians probably know how to make them. Ain't just mafia.)

Trieste. Northeast of Italy. The top of the Adriatic Sea.

(The Adriatic Sea has recently become known in the USA as well. Mickey Rourke – what's left of him – had a comeback party here. And Jack Nicholson before. Not to mention Meryl Streep.)

I was still sitting on the pier. All the drugs started to melt in my body. Giving me life, not an overdose.

(Irony. The real medication was irony.)

The whole city lay right in front of me. European cities lie, American cities stand, said Salvador Dali, a quite disgusting guy. Behind a European city there is another church, behind the American you'll find junkyards.

It wasn't noon yet, but already very hot. Hot summer smell: a mixture of sea, salt, traffic, spices from restaurants, rotten sea plants in the harbour. Mixed with a light breeze.

(And suddenly with an intense cloud of coffee scent. Later I found out why.)

I recognized (from the photos) the very city center: »*Piazza Unita d'Italia*« square.

Not as I expected. Different architecture: unlike Florence or Venice from the travel catalog images. No Italian stereotypes. Mostly House of Habsburg imperial Austrian style buildings, surrounded by Latin historical tradition with a lot of Slavic speech on the street. A New York echo.

(You expect »*Pasta Carbonara*« but you get »*Wienerschnitzel*«. – This is why I like Europe: the differences are genuine, historical. New York is, for comparison, a kind of zoo.)

The smell of coffee woke me up from my drug cocktail numbness.

One side of the *Piazza Unita* square was wide open – overlooking the sea and the harbor. I crossed the seaside promenade and slowly passed the buildings across the square. I didn't feel anything. I just desperately wanted coffee.

*Piazza Unita* was an imposing nineteenth century square full of people, with a large café on the left, but I decided not to have my first coffee there – I would have acted like a fucking tourist. And I definitely wasn't one.

I turned to the next street, a smaller square actually.

There was another café. Many cafés, full of people. Italians, mostly, talking to each other. Different from NYC-Italians: more bourgeois, nothing like Little Italy or Goodfellas. Without rich vulgarity but noble, posh in a more folkloric, historical way.

I watched people walking around. The way they walk. They had this European walk: it was a working day, but they didn't seem to be in a hurry at all. With different clothes, almost casual but elegant. Without the *I-have-to-make-a-million-today* expression on their faces.

I sat down in »*Caffé Portizza*« and ordered my first Italian coffee. I drank it in an instant as an alcoholic who swallows a whole bottle of whiskey right after returning from rehab.

My body came to life again.

(The last sentence is a typical oxymoron. My body will never come to life again. I wrote the sentence as it is, just to prove the significance of the irony. I took an almost suicidal amount of pills on the pier. They didn't kill me because irony overcomes logic. I must remember that.)

And then I saw something across the street. Something strange.

(The adjective »strange« ain't quite accurate. It would be acceptable for someone superstitious. But I don't give a fuck about superstition. Something is wrong: either adjective or reality.)

My next act is going to be a total failure. I do not use the word »mistake«. Mistakes can only satisfiy complete idiots: they use »mistakes« as a pathetic excuse for »being human«. I will not make a mistake, I will fail. We always fail, but at least we can try to fail better. »*To fail better*« ain't my idea – I borrowed it from Samuel Beckett.

My failure will be the following photo. A photo of what I saw across the street.

(You must never forgive me for my act. Just look at the fucking photo.)

In the twenty-first century, images dominate the world, not words. I used the image, but not to make some rotten compromise with the world. Irony made me do it. Irony teaches me. I try to understand the irony. If I fail, and I do and I always will, I can at least try to fail with brilliance: with the ultimate failure.

(Beckett's idea is revolutionary and scary. Because it clarifies the truth. Take advantage and use it.)

I didn't understand the slogan on the wall. I just took a photo.

In the past, I would ask myself, is this a coincidence? And my answer would be: of course it is, there is no such thing as predestination or fate. Don't fuck with me, I'm an atheist!

Now I wasn't sure. Not that I've become religious or at least superstitious lately, I'm more of an atheist than I've ever been before. I wasn't seeking for some signs. I saw the possibilities of interpretations, whether they were right or wrong. I stepped out of the black and white world.

(Gray. I discovered the color gray.)

I discovered the purpose of the »strange« inscription on the building: it was neither a coincidence nor a predestination.

It was a simple salute. The city knew me even before I arrived.

When I realized that cancer would soon be my death sentence, I ran away. Each destination seemed logical, possible or absolutely unacceptable at the same time. A total mess. But it was just a matter of time to leave. Wherever.

(Why I didn't stay in New York? – I could not. The fear was too strong. I had to move, even though I was never a travel freak. You move, you live: a pathetic, useless trick.)

The city of Trieste was a random choice.

The city of Trieste was the birthplace of my great-grandfather.

The city of Trieste had no sentimental value for me.

The city of Trieste was just an option, like a billion others.

The city of Trieste seemed like a complete failure.

Who the fuck has ever heard of the city of Trieste?

So I got enough arguments to choose Trieste.

(Eventually I figured out the meaning of the inscription on the building. It was about the past. I learned about the past. The past was the meaning. The eternal trap: the past. The past bothers us, not the future. The past is killing us. We are all past. We are all dead.)

My first Italian coffee at *Caffé Portizza* was espresso. Strong, bitter, velvety taste. I ordered another one and a cappuccino. All coffee along with all opioids was a great solution for introductory orientation problems. Suddenly, everything seemed clear. Perhaps it really was. Honestly, I don't remember quite well.

The waitress looked at me a little curiously.

"I'm American, you know? I wanna taste every good Italian coffee before I die."

(I told her the truth. Of course she didn't believe me.)

She answered something in Italian. I didn't understand a word she said. My Italian descent defines me less than that of all monkeys. I am an arrogant native English speaker. We believe the world is here to understand us. I smiled at her in apology.

She laughed and probably understood me. My smile. I didn't understand her and I liked her. Typically. We often like each other, but we rarely understand each other. So we run or kill. All life forms are basically trying to kill each other.

The cappuccino tasted good too. The name of the coffee was printed on the cup. I should have kept it in my mind. And I did. The brand was »*Illy*«.

I took another cigarette.

(No, I didn't quit smoking. The doctor warned me how smoking could worsen my medical condition. I explained to him that I would not be an organ donor after my death. No profit from my body available. He never said a word to me again. Not even hi-bye! Fucking vulgar protestant asshole.)

People around me were smoking. A release: it ain't illegal to smoke here on the street.

(I already checked this out in New York. It was a big plus for Trieste. My decision was an easy one. So it really wasn't my great-grandfather's fault that I moved to Trieste. Cigarettes are important, family is a burden.)

My pain comes in waves as well as fear. It was even worse in New York, more often. I do not create any illusions: death is inside me, walks with me, the shadow in the *Piazza Unita* – my shadow – wasn't really mine. Someone took me for a walk. I stepped into the darkness.

This is gonna be my last decision: I am ready to sell my soul to the devil.

In return I want to stand on my feet, I wanna walk, or swim straight to the end, meet the Master, laugh, go on, see, see the darkness, black eyes, yellow eyes, my blue eyes through the looking glass, I wanna feel death, taste, enjoy, never fall, disappear, disappear.

I do not gamble with my soul. I paid the bill. I bought a ticket. We have all been on the devil's playground for a very long time.

For eternity.

## CAT POWER: NOTHIN' BUT TIME

It's been a few days. I live. I'm home. Reading. Going out for a walk.

I rented a flat. I did it already in New York. The guy here – the landlord – was waiting for me. He gave me the keys and the contract. I paid the rent, half a year in advance. Life, real life is terribly easy and simple.

(Good to know before you die.)

The landlord didn't ask me anything at all except my impressions of the city.

"I fuckin' like it. I love it. I wanna die here."

Suddenly he got excited and started listing everything I should-could-have to visit... This poor bastard was really honest. He only saw a tourist. Stereotype.

Stereotypes are horror: first, because ninety percent (at least) are true and correct. But the remaining ten percent (if) are the ones that make life interesting. Ten percent break the rules, change the game, the ten percent is a place where you can breathe. If alive (ten percent, maybe), our species is on the run: because the game is boring, the rules are absurd, the reward in heaven is literally a blasphemy.

I let the guy finish his speech and show me the apartment. He didn't ask me why I was here, God bless, because if he did, I would tell him the truth, I swear. And ruin his life. I know that, I've seen it before. Not just once. The truth is too hard to swallow. Nobody wants that. People want fiction, fairytales, myths, anything but the truth. Any artificial mental construct is necessary for the organization of society.

I didn't want to hurt or offend my landlord and his sunny empathy, but I stopped him. I asked him about the inscription I saw on arrival.

He began to explain something, but in the historical context his English was poor. Like, obviously, all Italians, he used all parts of his body more than his tongue.

The end of WW2, allies (his arms left and right), Italy versus Communists, mamma mia! (his head towards the sky), Treaty of Peace with Italy, United Nations (head down, praying hands), East – West border (mamma mia! again), tension, danger, USA, Winston Churchill, lots of alcohol (more gestures, more hands, more eyebrows). Fucked up scene.

(OK. Got it: I'm welcome. Thank you. Bye!)

He left. I looked around: forty-five m², one large room, kitchen, bathroom, balcony. Furniture included. »*Borgo Teresiano*« district, downtown, fourth floor, seven hundred euros per month.

(*Borgo Teresiano* was named after Maria Theresa, the Austrian-Habsburg monarch. Trieste became part of Italy only in 1920, after the end of the First World War and the collapse of Austro-Hungarian monarchy. The furniture in the apartment stylistically corresponded to the Habsburg period. Extinct centuries. I stepped again, similar to the ocean, into the dead zone.)

After a few days and the feeling of being at home, I knew: this is where I will tell the story.

Of course, this is an act of pure vanity. For the living and especially for the dead. We disappear, the universe will not miss us.

But we do it anyway. Silence is our enemy. A French writer I like tried to explain why:

*»When the grave lies open before us, let's not try to be witty, but on the other hand, let's not forget, but make it our business to record the worst of the human viciousness we've seen without changing one word. When that's done, we can curl up our toes and sink into the pit. That's work enough for a lifetime.«*

This is a toxic explanation, but it may be true. I took deep in my consciousness his next piece of advice: »*The beginning of genius is being scared shitless.«*

I'm scared shitless and therefore I am a genius to tell you this.

(»Genius« can be put in quotation marks, but not as a quote. Just with all the emphasis on »scared shitless«.)

My story won't be just full of quotes. The world itself is a quote if you try to understand it. Because you're not, you're certainly not the first pathetic moterfucker trying to understand.

Remember all those behind you. They are great company. They talk to you, you can listen. Remember your kind, whether they are dead or not. They will never let you down.

People do not remember, they don't want to remember. Each generation believes that the universe began on the day of their birth. Remembering is meaningles to them. Because there is nothing to remember if they weren't there. History does not exist. The human race keeps repeating the same mistakes over and over again. The pharaohs did the same as we do, only they didn't drive a car. The alibi for doing so is the cult of immortality. Immortality – a miserable and endlessly stupid belief. The oldest, largest and longest-running corporation of all time – the Roman Chatolic Church – has built its vulgar wealth on this endlessly stupid belief. The best-selling product of all time is immortality, not some shitty software. The price is huge: the more you believe, the more fear awaits you in the end.

Remeber all those behind you. They are some damn great company. Take advantage and fuck your own past, forget about the future, there is none. The dead will help, you can trust them, they have absolutely no reason to lie. So take another quote. Choose your own nation.

(Never forget the irony! My God – he prefers the term »coffee friend« because I'm an atheist – is coming around soon: you could invite him to a good Italian coffee. He'll tell you another killing joke.)

Dying is the reason why I could write a story. Even a novel. An American novel.

Perhaps every single man wants to tell a story. Only a few can do it. It's a very, very thin line between telling a story and using language as escapism. Lack of words is not a reason for defeat, it's quite the opposite: people use too many words, they talk permanently, with one and only intention – to talk. To fill the empty space, to eliminate fear. Officially, we call this »small talk«. In fact, it is not small, but heavily inflated. People talk not to explain, but to avoid fear. To die long before they face death.

Language has become the most important form of escapism in the modern world, even more fatal than the holy escapist trinity religion-sport-pornography.

(I'm not sure, but maybe Facebook has already replaced pornography.)

Silence is a rare event. It requires knowledge and courage. Creating a story means reducing words, not adding redundant ones.

And here's the trick: being clear means approaching silence. You have to be brave to do that. Because what's left is your risk: you make a leap into the darkness and hope you haven't lost your path.

(If you fail, and you do, you fall. Stay on the ground. It hurts. Listen to the silence. The next word may help you get up. This is not a promise. Perhaps you'll just fail like a jerk and die like an asshole.)

This is where I will tell the story.

*Borgo Teresiano* is my home now. No doubt. No coincidences. The past is gone; time ain't your enemy; avoid linear thinking; observe fear.

*Borgo Teresiano* must be a place without lies. Nothing less, nothing more.

Maybe I can write a story now because I'm dying. When you're dying, lies cannot be involved. The story becomes significant only without lying.

I lied before. I was only lying. My whole life has been a lie. This is not surprising: lies are the only truth in most people's lives. A lie is a paradigm. Not just in Western civilization, this is the paradigm of humanity: avoiding fear with lies.

(Because fear – like stupidity – is democratic: fear is not a choice of gender, age, race, nation, religion, whatever. This is why democracy is the only justified political system. Unfortunately, fear and stupidity prevail. If you buy a toothpick, you are warned that it is not primarily intended to scratch someone's eyes out of the skull. The irony of democracy: idiots rule. Plato laughs in his grave.)

I was a ghostwriter, a copywriter, name it as-you-want-writer. I was anything but a writer. I was paid to tell lies, very well paid. I wrote dialogues, speeches, slogans, commercials. Disgusting stuff. My speech for a local politician was much more expensive than a blowjob for this same politician (although, I guess, he spent a lot more money on blowjobs).

I was just a very expensive whore (considering the low price of a blowjob, not my actual earnings).

I was a writing ghost on his way to become a real ghost.

So now I'm in a hurry. Soon I will be a real ghost, and before this happens, I have to tell the truth. I cannot die in a lie.

(Beautiful rhyme, a soothing one.)

I do not expect anyone to be interested in my so-called truth. I have nothing to explain, I have no wisdom to preach, I just have to die and it will happen within words.

I am now forty-nine years old. When I was younger, much younger, I wrote some poems. Noble opposition to my actual work, I thought. Of course, they were pure bullshit. I was so infinitely naive: at the time, I thought poetry was a powerful expression. Later, I realized that almost all contemporary poetry is just a more pathetic lie, used by narcissistic egocentric maniacs that create astonishing tornadoes of their souls in a cup of tea. Besides, poetry is practical: it doesn't require much time or work. Compared to poetry, even copywriting is a decent job.

(Beware of poets today: those sick aggressive psychopaths often like weapons and call for slaughter in the name of universal harmony.)

Literature – on the contrary – is a slow, arduous, lonely and cruel activity, with no promises other than hard work. This is how it should be: the price is the highest and the profit uncertain if there is any at all.

The »poetic« experience was short-lived, brutal failure. It had one positive side effect: I never published any of that crap. I was ashamed for writing it, but proud to have thrown it in the toilet. Brutal failure without brilliance, but at least with a drop of style.

(Failure: measuring device without units. You can measure despair, count your pathetic actions. After a while, you wonder what else you can totally fuck up. When you are able to ask yourself this question, you feel a little better.)

It's been a few days.

My vow was: I'll never use any transportation. Just walk. Trieste is not such a big city: population of about 200.000 people. I bought myself a new pair of elegant sandals. These boots are made for walking.

The very first walk out, the first morning in Trieste was a complete surprise.

»*Canal Grande*« is the center of my district. Let there be no misunderstanding: the »*Grand Canal*« in Venice is not the same thing. My canal in *Borgo Teresiano* is literally a dead end. Blind alley. Cul-de-sac. A tongue of the sea licking the city. About three hundred meters long, it ends in front of the »*Piazza Sant' Antonio Nuovo*« square.

(I said »meters«, not yards. I am trying to adopt the European metric system.)

I sat down at »*Caffe Le Vele*« and ordered both: espresso and cappuccino.

(»*Americana*« – black coffee with some extra cold water was also on the menu. Too banal to drink it.)

A bridge was built across the canal, two bridges actually. On the first one, which was now in front of me, just a few steps away, I saw a fixed silhouette and some – I assumed – tourists around it. I finished my espresso, left my things and cappuccino on the table, and went to look at it. When I got closer, I found the monument: a life-size human figure.

It was James Joyce.

There was an inscription on the memorial plaque: »*La mia anima è a Trieste*«, *1909, A Letter to Nora.* My soul is in Trieste, he wrote this to his wife Nora, his lifelong wife and partner.

You're kidding me, I thought. I'm in Joyce's town? The irony obviously has something to do with this, not coincidence.

I went back to my table (no, nothing was stolen) and checked Joyce's biography on my cell phone. Meanwhile, tourists hugged the statue and took photos.

(Horrible thing. A bronze statue cannot say GO FUCK YOURSELF!)

The facts were clear: James Joyce lived in Trieste for a really long time after leaving Ireland. He found a job here, nowhere else. Teaching English, writing Ulysses. I had no idea. I knew he lived abroad (Paris, Switzerland), not in Ireland. He hated Ireland. »*A race of clodhoppers*« was his compliment to his fellow countrymen. If the writer lives abroad, it is supposed to be Paris, not Trieste.

(With the exception of French writers: they flee Paris.)

Other information about Joyce in Trieste was: »*Passaggio Joyce*« (pedestrian walkway), »*Museo Joyce*« (museum), »*Caffe James Joyce*« (café) and »*Caffe Stella Polare*« (Joyce's favorite café in Trieste).

I read Joyce. I read the damn Ulysses – the most famous book in the world that nobody reads. He exaggerated with the technique, indeed, but you cannot skip the radicalism of ideas, the avant-garde of his personal liberation, the gigantic influence, horror to all conservatives. A total denial of social hypocricy. »*You talk to me of nationality, language, religion. I shall try to fly by those nets.«* For such a statement, he would have been burned at the stake some century earlier.

(I am seriously afraid – a hundred years after his death, the punishment could be the same again.)

His writing basically meant FUCK YOU! to the whole world. Some kind of punk in literature.

(Or is it more Captain Beefheart alike?)

If copy– or ghostwriter, you are definitely learning from authors like him. He invented all the tricks there are.

(No wonder: Joyce's »Ulysses« character in the novel, Leopold Bloom, is actually an advertising agent.)

You can hardly read the novel he wrote, but the eruption of ideas is endless. And you use it for some bullshit commercial while Japanese (oops... Chinese?) tourists hug the inventor's monument.

Now, of course, you understand the perverse state of the helpless, sodomized bronze statue on the bridge.

*Caffe Le Vele* was almost empty. I should have made a toast to Joyce, but I haven't drank alcohol in quite some time, years actually. Not because of my illness – cancer had nothing to do with it. I replaced the substances that I occasionally use. A matter of style, not a moral decision.

(And now – opioids are both: a matter of style and a matter of pain. Pain wins and breaks you, but you can at least try to drop dead with elegance. In shiny shoes.)

Joyce was a heavy drinker for some time.

Addiction is a secret. Addiction is a vulgar pleasure. Addiction is a religion. Addiction is a dangerous border to the other side. Addiction is the risk that you need to take seriously at least once in your lifetime. Addiction can swallow you and make you a piece of shit. Addiction gives you life or death.

Addiction is gambling for idiots. Addiction is a solution for those who know they'll fail.

Addiction is a game where you can bet only with your soul. (Well known procedure: Faust did it in Europe, Robert Johnson in America. After all – it's the only bet there is.)

Of course, you can decide otherwise: stay forever young, as the billboards command you. You choose a healthy lifestyle (what the fuck is that?), vegetables, running, hugging trees, talking to ghosts (literally), using a seat belt in the toilet, fresh breakfast smoothies, pink lipstick at the age of ninety.

(In recent decades, literature has become the same: nowadays authors go vegan, not drunk. Their sentences remind me of the water supply system in India's slums.)

I just finished my two coffees. And I was going to order whiskey for the crazy Irish too (I wouldn't drink, but bless the *Canal Grande* with it) when... Well, there's always a moment in your life when things suddenly go terribly wrong.

Like for example: you are informed that you are seriously ill and you're gonna die soon. But there are also worse things.

Like for example: »*Hotel California*« on the radio. Sweet fuckin' Jesus, does the whole world really still listen to this wannabe rock puke? Desperate housewives satisfaction?

(Sometimes death is better, not only in Pet Sematary.)

Torture quickly became unbearable. I left the money with a tip on the table and ran away.

I chose rock'n'roll to be the sound for the dead. So be it. There are many misunderstandings in this context. Fucking a python on stage ain't necessarily rock'n'roll; nor is describing the KKK as a charity; showing tits on TV can be done without sound.

(Or being fat, goddamnit. You can't be fat and claim to be

rock'n'roll at the same time. How is it even possible for any of these drug addicts to become a fat fuck? The combination of MDMA and cocaine can make you look like PR for Auschwitz in two weeks. And by the way: Henry Rollins is not included in this immoral statistics.)

I walked along the canal, found the pedestrian walkway (which is in fact just a narrow bridge over the canal), went back to the monument and... And than the pain came back. Fear came back. I interrupted my Joyce-excursion and returned back home. My books were there.

»*It was amazing, even, to think that the only thing left to people in their despair was reading.*«

(Said another French writer I like. You can quite often trust French writers.)

Awareness of death erupted with volcanic fury. I grabbed my books, I grabbed words and sentences like a life belt.

Does writing begin in the realm of fear and death?

Fyodor Dostoevsky was sentenced to death and already standing in front of the firing squad; the tsar commuted the sentence a few seconds before the execution.

Are »*Brothers Karamazov*« possible only after death?

Experience is necessary, as is weakness. Weakness may be the key. When you're down, on your knees, helpless, you have two choices: either you start praying or you try to understand. Dostoevsky combined the two. My way of understanding is not so monumental.

Literature ain't no product of power, it is the result of fear and self-doubt. So I let my weakness to be my guidance. I try to clean existential stains with epistemological impotence.

(No sane person would write the last sentence. I did it to demonstrate a disastrous failure.)

This is where I will tell the story.

Time is gone, I'm alone, scared shitless, without ambition. I remember nothing. Riding with death makes you the loneliest person in the world. You will die alone, you know that, and it's a good thing. You know, or hope, now you can find the words. Your story will be a failure, so it may not be too long.

I recalled my second literary experiment, after poetry. It was the idea of such an impressive, unusual, brand new story (there are no brand new stories, you stupid asshole!), a story so great that it could astonish. Literature itself. I just had to find a story like that. So I did some sort of truman-capote-research on a newspaper article.

There was this guy who stole the corpse of his dead girlfriend from the morgue. Not a pervert necrophile or a crime – he just wanted to lie next to her for a while.

At first I thought I won the lottery.

I failed again. I had to, I'm an American. Formalities are irrelevant. What happens in »*Crime and Punishment*«? – Some guy kills an old woman. Nothing exceptional. A miserable plot, but a remarkable story.

(I was ashamed: do I really need half a century of life to realize something so simple?)

My confession was simple: what I do is rape. I raping words, I raping reality. But fear brought me access – ironically – to a language I had never known before.

A story about fear may seem boring. But it's not my story. It's our story. And you'll be scared shitless too, I promise.

# BRUCE SPRINGSTEEN: A NIGHT WITH THE JERSEY DEVIL

I sleep well here. I didn't in New York. The shock caused by the disease was too irritating. Everything is just about one single second. The second when you read the sentence from your diagnosis. Your life lasts one second. I'm sure Einstein would agree.

I read THE SENTENCE, two words to be exact, in less than a second.

The funny thing was: I didn't feel any fear at all. I smiled.

(I would never have believed that such a reaction was possible. But it really happened, I swear.)

The fear came later. After a week or two I realized: I have to leave New York urgently. There's too much life in New York, but I had to reduce, remove life. I recognized the paradox: if I am alone, the fear begins to melt a little. A mystery emerges. So just drink it up.

(This paradox was neither a paradox nor a possibility of consciousness. It was a simple fact. A surprising fact. Irony.)

I tried to trace that absurd smile of mine. Where did it come from? Reading was the only solution I had.

»*Only literature can grant you access to a spirit from beyond the grave – a more direct, more complete, deeper access than you'd have in conversation with a friend.*«

(Said a trustworthy French writer I like. I believe him. I was more and more convinced that there are no fucking coincidences at all. Why did precisely the French leave both Americas?)

I tried to trace that absurd smile of mine.

Not in New York, not in damn Paris, not in Florence or Venice or Rome. Fear was my guidance. When you're scared shitless, you see countless possibilities, not just one crossroad. I smiled because all of them made sense. It was irony that made me smile. I needed NOTHING. Trieste did not exist: at least 7.500.000.000 of the world's nearly eight billion people had never heard of it. Trieste was not. A perfect choice for not to be.

At seven thirty a.m. I was on the street, almost in a hurry. Outside I greeted Joyce on the bridge – it's nice to have a friend like that first thing in the morning.

Two minutes later, I was sitting at a table at the »*James Joyce Caffe*«. I ordered espresso and cappuccino as if it were my lifelong habit. The waiter didn't care, I was the only guest.

»*Espresso-è-cappuccino-prego!*« became something new: the birth of the task.

The decision or definition was simple: I will name the task »Cappuccino Odyssey«. Given the fact that Joyce had a distinct sense of humor, I assumed that »*old father, old artificer*« would not resent my paraphrase.

Cappuccino Odyssey cannot be an ambitious project. Drinking coffee, taking opioids and waiting for death will not change an entire century. It won't change the language either. But it will confirm the irony. That's enough.

*James Joyce Caffe* was absolutely not a souvenir place: nothing like Irish interior, no photos of Joyce, no Joyce's breakfast on the menu. I'm quite sure the young waiter had no idea who the fuck Joyce was.

It was just a regular working day with people drinking

coffee in the morning. I did the same. Cappuccino Odyssey began.

(It started a long time ago. I wasn't aware of that. How the hell could a native New Yorker even imagine not to die in Manhattan?)

My great-grandfather left Trieste in 1918 after the catastrophic defeat of the Italian army at the Battle of Caporetto in the First World War.

As a proud Italian nationalist, he could not bear the humiliation. To be honest: he was a fascist and a racist as well. Coming to the United States would give him back some dignity. Standing on Ellis Island he left his shame behind. He chose his new American name and became a pure white supremacist, supporting Mussolini, Hitler and the KKK for the next few decades until he died. He was a real New Yorker because he came from somewhere else.

One century later I am standing on the domestic soil of the old idiotic motherfucker. It's the end of the road. The meaning is similar to Aristotle's catharsis: bring the shit to where it belongs.

(And clean it!)

I left my name behind. I don't need it any more. I am not. No time, no personal names. Trieste stays, I do not. Death does not require identification of any kind. The final step forward is speechless and nameless.

The Last Judgement should not raise great expectations, because God is alive and bored, infinitely bored. He absolutely doesn't give a fuck about his own creation, I know him well enough to claim that.

And I don't envy him: he's the most desperate creature in the entire universe. With no other option but to exist. I believe he would kill himself right away, stop the nonsence, bring us real salvation, stay dead... but he can't – people would give him thousands, millions of lives over and over again.

Nietzsche's god has never been more alive. Doubts have been raised in the past. Not now. God is a hostage of eternity and has nothing to exchange for his desired death.

(I feel sorry for him, I honestly do. I can only imagine the horror: he invented coffee, but not the joy of drinking it. This is his punishment: he failed the best.)

In the square to my left there was a huge white plastic rabbit (maybe it was plastic, maybe some other material, who cares) – some kind of sculptural installation. The image was bizarre: a quietly sitting rabbit was surrounded by aristocratic villas, some of them as posh as possible, some almost in ruins. The grotesque rabbit couldn't have fit the place better.

This was the exact moment of strange awareness: for the very first time I recognized it, even though it was so obvious: »IT« was a combination. A combination of greatness and disintegration. There were buildings, majestic buildings, almost like those in ancient Greece or Rome, like the Parthenon. And postapocalyptic ruins across the street. This was the exact moment of something so clear and logical. Something I haven't noticed yet.

(How the hell haven't I seen this before? – This was the story of the whole West. And above all, this was the story of the USA, not just Trieste.)

I'm being stupid, no matter how hard I try to avoid mistakes.

(Idiot! I used the word »mistake«!)

I'm stupid because I've always tried to act logically, to use notorious common sense, whatever that means.

Now I know: to be intelligent means to be abstract, not logical.

(There is no logic in human society. Our actions are mostly suicidal. What kind of logic is that?)

I left the money on the table, ate the pills (not because of the pain), drank all the water in the glass and left. My next destination was nearby: »*Stella Polare Caffe*«. Joyce's favorite place in Trieste.

In the square, I walked past the Jefferson-Airplane-White-Rabbit sculpture and almost took a photo as proof that it really exists.

(But I didn't. That means: for the first time I didn't fail. Why would I need evidence for anyone? The damn rabbit exists, believe it or not – it's your fucking problem, not mine.)

*Stella Polare Caffe* is not really spectacular these days. An ordinary café with a memorial plaque on the wall explaining that Joyce was often here with his close Italian friend and writer Italo Svevo.

Tables: plastic imitations of rattan. Chairs: plastic imitations of rattan. Made in? – Guess three times.

(Let me help you: ain't Armani or Versace. So there is only one option left.)

I bet the furniture was different a hundred years ago. Plastic chairs, the Parthenon and the ruins side by side, black street vendors (probably illegal refugees) with their cheap crap of any kind, elegance and dirt in the *Canal Grande*, elegant people and some dirty addicts on a long coastal promenade, the white rabbit, languages you don't understand – yes, this is the twenty-first century, this is our – Western – decadence par excellence.

Palm trees were growing right at the end of the *Canal Grande*. Together with the white rabbit, they represented psychedelia of a very special kind. Jim Morrison should find this place and not damn Paris like everyone usually does. Unlike me, he could even survive here. But he chose poetry and Paris – in this case, the last stop can only be the Père Lachaise cemetery. Of-course-and-it-goes-without-saying-etc-and-so-on, poetry is to blame.

(The above-mentioned hypothesis about the murderous effects of poetry can be easily proved: my death, for example, will be caused by a killing joke. Strictly genre-wise, a joke is by no means poetry.)

My espresso & cappuccino were on the table. And sudden awareness: the exact moment of the next – very pleasant – awareness: there were women all around, Italian (I heard them talking) in their middle years, forties or fifties or even more. They all looked beautiful.

I will definitely not be vulgar and use the imbecil pornographic abbreviation for this type. Because these are not what they are. It was peace in their gestures, a truly feminine joy, very sexy but not cheap. Quite the opposite: elegant and – most importantly – with obvious self-confidence, no matter how old they really are, without any form of being pathetic. You don't see that in America. In America, an eighty-year-old-pink-lipstick-creature will try to imitate teenagers and behave like a whore.

(By the way: Jane Fonda is not included in this immoral statistics. She is smart and intelligent and therefore beautiful.)

How could I get closer to one of them? Say hello, invite for a drink, make up some other total bullshit like that? Or just simply approach and suggest a very-very-very slow fuck before I die? Or rather to jerk off at home?

Honestly? – I'm not in the mood. I don't miss sex much.

My very-very-very special lady in the long black veil I'm fucking with right now is exhausting me without even touching her.

Nevermind: I had a nice view. I've always liked older women, even in my younger days. Young chicks have no imagination, no secrets, only their bodies in a hurry. Eroticism is hidden in our brains, to discover it, we need time. And use brain. That is why sexy begins only after forty.

Someone tapped me on the shoulder. It was time. I was expecting him. The waitress brought him coffee, black as usual. He looked at me and smiled.
- I assume you've been watching women?
- Yes, I was.
- You should. They really are a divine creation.
- From my point of view, yes, they are.
- And what is your point of view?
- Well... heterosexual, I guess...
- Hmm. Please don't be offended, but I strongly disagree. Currently, your point of view is, among other attractions, including women, *Canal Grande*!
- It is... of course. I'm just talking about sexual orientation...
- Groase! What a definition! Orientation? About what? What's left or right? Up or down? I wonder who invented such geographical nonsense...
- They say ... you did.
- Holy shit! Who are they?
- Well... they... people. People who... worship you...
- They talk too much and above all they have no idea what they are talking about in the first place.
- They say you say what's right or wrong.

- Indeed! I do. I say: geography is one term, sex is another one. Are you following me?
- I hope so...
- Can I ask you one simple question?
- Please do.
- Is there a male person you'd say damn – he looks good! Oh, and pardon my language, please!
- Well... yes, there is.
- But you're talking to me about the so-called heterosexual point of view?
- Fuck...
- Do not bother, please. I just wanted to see you. To see how do you dive into this city. And the coffee here is great, you noticed?
- »To dive« is a cruel verb.
- No shit? Are you trying to be sentimental?
- No. My attempt was to be sarcastic. But of course I failed.
- I know.
- Why?
- Because you like to dive. You adore diving. You dive all your life so... close to...
- Is there any chance not to respect you?
- »Respect« is a cruel noun. Suppose you can't ignore me. Only honest atheists never ignore me.
- Why are you talking to me?
- Because you listen. Not just listen to me, of course, you listen everywhere and to everyone. And please don't take this as an insult. I respect your atheist position.
- Motherfucker...
- Ha, ha, ha... a strong word. I like it! So... do you feel

comfortable in your new home?
- I do. Should I thank you for the advice?
- My advice? Jesus fucking... oh... my language again, excuse me... I didn't give you any advice! You do have free will, remember? And that's not a divine concept, wouldn't you agree?
- But... you should... supervise everything. Don't you?
- Oh, please... don't be such a naive idiot. Just look at poor Jesus! Paul the Apostle transformed his teaching beyond recognition. And what do I have to do with it?
- Well... he, Jesus, should be your...
- Don't even go there! I never claimed he was my son. I don't mess around with virgins. You see – we have something interesting in common!
- We have?
- Look around! All the women you just admired!
- Bullshit! You are immortal. How could you possibly be a fan of middle-aged women?
- Why not? It's just a matter of sophisticated taste.
- So you didn't...
- ... fuck a virgin? Absolutely not. Defloration is a job for cowards and psychopaths. Damn – this coffee really is great! Have I already apologized for my language?
- You have. But tell me about Jesus...
- There's nothing more to tell. I told you about Paul the Apostle. What else do you need to know? Besides: Paul's enterprise is much bigger than me. That's why I constantly hear some false accusations about how bad editor-in-chief I am.
- You're not so bad?
- I'm no editor at all.

From my point of view, I saw the *Canal Grande*. My

coffee friend was right. How could he be wrong anyway?

I turned around, took a new pack of cigarettes from my bag and in the meantime he was gone, vanished from my sight. I decided to enjoy my point of view a little more and smoke a little more because I wasn't supposed to be killed by lung cancer.

You can't smoke freely in New York. You can't drink coffee and have a cigarette without moral obligations in New York.

(»*Smoke gets in your eyes*«, but not in a free country.)

My country is dying. Tobacco is the ultimate enemy, one of thousands of them. When you're scared, scared shitless, you fight all potential enemies, no matter how fictional they are. You become insane and try to avoid any danger. You accuse, if necessary, tobacco as well. A crusade against tobacco will save the country, the soul of the country.

(Explain that to Humphrey Bogart.)

Perhaps only a few inventions in history can prove that there is any meaning in this world. Coffee and cigarettes reach the top three. Coffee and cigarettes make sense. They kill, of course, but so does milkshake.

New York was disappearing so fast that I could no longer activate any memories. As if I was really trying... I wasn't homesick. I started with a new task – Cappuccino Odyssey. And forgot one thing: I should keep some statistics on the coffee brand. They are so many. Why not organize a Coffee Olympics?

Cappuccino Odyssey wasn't tricky enough to erase the fear. The fear not only vanished like my coffee friend, it was stable and when it became unbearable, I took opioids. It was medicine after all. Medicine should keep you alive. Opioids kept me alive, no doubt about it.

(Yes, yes, yes, your guess is correct – I thought about it a lot: just take too much, much too much and end the agony! But somehow I felt there was a betrayal lurking in the suicide. If my coffee friend ain't no fucking editor, whose hint was that?)

I finally left *Stella Polare*. On the way, I stopped at a tobacco shop and checked the newspapers. The New York Times was there. I bought it even though I was an online subscriber.

There is something sexy about paper. I couldn't remember the last time I held a PAPER daily newspaper in my hand. I should be careful now not only with words but also with the materials. You wanna fuck an artificial doll or smell one small piece of real skin instead?

The paper is exciting because it has a character. The book is the oldest medium in the world and still ongoing. Eternal love and lust.

I didn't give a shit about the news, especially not for the ones from New York. There is no news: throughout history, people have fought exclusively for one and the only »correct« interpretation of the world. The monopoly over interpretation is all that matters, it rules human society. So the news has been the same since the Stone Age.

I piss my pants laughing every time I hear the phrase »the situation is complicated«. This world is old enough and boring even more. But not complicated. The simplicity is stunning. *»Simplicity is always the secret, to a profound truth, to doing things, to writing, to painting. Life is profound in its simplicity«* as the brilliant drunk Charles Bukowski claims.

I returned back home with The New York Times and groceries from Eataly Market – the same store as Flatiron on

5th Avenue and Eataly Downtown in the Financial District. The world has long since become global indeed.

I never really paid attention to my Italian ancestry, even my father no longer spoke Italian. (And I learned a few words – *si, va bene* – from the Godfather movies.)

Honestly, the food at Flatiron was kinda cool, so I used to be an occasional customer there.

My appetite has never reached the Himalayan heights, especially not now, but I was able to eat some »*acciughe con capperi e boboli*« and use The Times as a placemat, an elegant tool, just like women's linguerie.

(No blasphemy, no insults – just another proof about paper being sexy. If being sexy means: you are absolutely not vulgar, but almost painfully desirable at the same time.)

The store – Eataly – is the same in Manhattan as in Trieste. What makes the difference? I'm pretty sure, it's an abstract past, not people. Differences are an abstract product with a concrete form. People don't think much about their behavior, they just know it's the only right one. The past is hunting us, death is the only escape.

Why are women different in Trieste? – Because they don't run. The past, their past ain't a burden, just a fact.

I'm American. Is there any special feature that describes an American today? – I would say: decline and fall.

(This was the exact moment of strange, almost scary awareness. It was so obvious again. »IT« appeared again. »IT« a combination of greatness and disintegration.)

Decline and fall is the true face of the American Dream. American Dream is just a liberal or libertarian idea, an extreme conservative dogma, the greatest and most important myth about American society. And like all myths, it has nothing to do with reality. In ancient Egypt, Pharaoh was God with his divine rights. Millions have died for the divine myth and some pyramids remained. Decline and fall is American contemporary reality. One person in a million actually succeeds, all the others are collateral damage to maintain the myth. You can decline and fall a billion times. And you'll do it again, one last time, forever. Americans die, always, for myth only. This is a source of our political power: we don't care about reality, we keep inventing an artificial one. The USA is fiction. We can die in Vietnam, Iraq or Afghanistan for one big fuckin' nothing. We die for fiction. Our fiction has a name: business as usual. Millions have died for our fiction and what remains is... the Empire State Building.

(I hope.)

Decline and fall means death to me. Decline and fall for my country means: the show is over. We are now performing B-sides material if anyone wants to listen.

(»The B-sides« playlist is an optimistic solution considering a totally fucked up band.)

Strange awareness was a moment of clarity: Trieste may be in the same position. The combination of greatness and disintegration equals American decline and fall. Italian Detroit. With a significant difference: the decline and fall in Trieste will happen with style. It's the Roman Empire tradition present around here.

The perfect place for an American to die.

I came home quite some time ago. I didn't eat or drink much, mostly I was looking for sentences.

(I explain this to all hard-science-obsessed readers who believe in what they were told in school: food or drink is the basis of our survival. A skeptical intellectual reader would add oxygen too. Only a few doubt it. And therefore lose hunger or thirst.)

Evenings can be tough: despair floods your body with pain and anxiety attacks. These are moments of horror, moments of unbearable absurdity – maybe I should just »take too much« after all.

You see who you are: you see »*isolation, abandonment, fear and anxiety – all of the high points of one's life*«.

(As described by the quite famous and never sentimental »English fag«.)

You know, you are clearly aware: the nation of the dead keeps you alive. Irony won't let you die yet.

I'm afraid of the evenings. So I came up with a trick: I take all the books out of a cardboard suitcase and bring them to the balcony. The authors are (almost) all dead people. And I can see long-dead Joyce on the bridge.

I beg them, dead and mighty, to help me. I'm such a fucking coward.

»*Now you are going to die. Don't worry. I am here. I won't let you sink. Go on with your reading.*«

(This answer came to me from a French writer I like. Since he is one of the living, I wondered if he could be scared shitless too? I seriously doubt it. I think he's died several times already. Now he can piss on his own grave with liberating satisfaction.)

I didn't eat or drink much, the evening was still hot, the summer was at its peak. I found an interesting information: the ancient Egyptian god Thoth was the god of writing and the god of the dead as the same divine entity.

(Another sign that could trace that absurd smile of mine?)

I know I'm gonna die soon. But that's not the point. The point ain't sacred, on the contrary, it is profane. The consequence is simple: people mostly choose faith and the promised eternal life. Denial of death degenerates into grotesque: irony prevails. Jesus dies, God is silent. I'm beginning to understand my coffee friend.

God is all around us, it must be, for most people it is the only solution. When I left *Stella Polare Caffe,* I went past the Serbian Orthodox Church with some unknown writings to me. I took photos to check the inscriptions at home. So I did: the writing was Old Church Slavic, very old, I could study it a little more, but suddenly I felt too much of God's presence in my apartment.

I rather recalled all the women from *Stella Polare.* I begged them, alive and beautiful, to help me fall asleep. To sink deep as I have in the middle of the ocean.

The sky, the smell, the night over Trieste heard my prayer. From my balcony I watched through the night across the sea.

Sometimes I hear a gentle, kind laugher behind my back. More like a whisper. Even though it's behind my back, I feel like it's coming from the sea.

At this point, I can go to sleep.

## COP SHOOT COP: ROOM 429

*»Sunday morning, brings the dawn in ...«*

The promenade by the sea was full of people. Another giant cruise ship was anchored in front of *Piazza Unita* square. *Costa Luminosa* was her name. I checked out her route: a week-long Mediterranean round trip. Otherwise she sails to South America, all the way down to Tierra del Fuego, near penguins in Antarctica.

(Isn't it weird to mention those penguins so often?)

*»It's just a restless feeling by my side...«*

Sitting on the bench a few feet away, I curiously watched the ship. Is there a chance that among the nearly eight billion people, one will step off the ship on a pier, just like me, sit down on a bench and I could read from his or her face that...

No way! The ship came from Genoa. People from Genoa do not come to die or kill themselves in Trieste. For such a purpose they would use the Golden Gate Bridge in San Francisco.

*»Sunday morning and I'm falling...«*

My intention that day was not to be a guide for some desperate motherfucker anyway. It was Sunday morning. I wanted to visit the church. One was close: *»San Nicolo«* – the other Orthodox, Greek Orthodox this time.

(Legend claims – Joyce's favorite...)

*»I've got a feeling I don't want to know...«*

I got in. There was some renovation going on; the left side

of the church was under construction, but the mass was regularly scheduled. I found a priest, very young, standing next to me. I wanted to ask him about a mass – is it Orthodox? Is a white-Anglo-Saxon-Protestant-atheist presence a blasphemy? Is it even allowed?

He did not speak English.

(He did NOT speak English. So there are still miracles in this world, or at least in the Catholic world. God himself is supposed to be polyglot. At least in the New Testament. But who gives a fuck about the New Testament in America? America owns the Babel Tower from the Old Testament. There is only one divine language left.)

And then I heard... fuck me! – Gregorian chant!

The overture was beautiful, but after a few minutes the damn priest started with his pedophile-type of singing. It was as exciting as the »*Hotel California*«. I escaped immediately.

(There may have been ten people in the church. Maybe one of them was a true believer. Maybe the priest really was a pedophile. Maybe the next, the Ecclesiastical Empire, now sees decline and fall. And maybe only the Sistine Chapel remains.)

I hid in some backstreet. Cafés everywhere, even here. One would think that coffee is the only economy around.

(As a matter of fact – it almost is. The baseline report on this topic follows exclusively for my potential readers of the Wall Street Journal who are not interested in dying because they will never die.)

Cappuccino Odyssey, next chapter: »*Caffe Pep's*«, Illy coffee brand. I started drinking black espresso and cappuccino with sugar. Reason? No reason. Irony.

Next to my table, a large red elephant tried to push the building in front of him a little more further. He may have been a plastic elephant, but he was certainly a companion to the white rabbit. Not to mention I also met a bunch of pink wolves and a red fucking plastic frog climbing up the building. I'm sure, they were all part of the same gang.

(Andy Warhol would love it. And contribute a polar bear – yellow? – with boxing gloves.)

A cup (or better: a small glass) of coffee in Trieste is a deadly serious phenomenon. Italy introduced coffee culture to the rest of the world. Trieste has long been the center of the coffee trade in Italy: »coffee city«, the main »coffee port«. The tradition dates back to the Austrian era. Clouds of coffee smell in the air. Espresso and cappuccino and macchiato came to the USA from Trieste. Go west, my fellow American, and visit the famous »*Caffe Trieste*« in San Francisco!

(Readers of the Wall Street Journal obviously do not know where the fuck Trieste is. If they had known, the entire coffee industry here would have collapsed decades ago.)

A woman in black, my age, sat alone at a table near me. I smiled to myself. She was alive. I'm alive. When I die, she disappears, not me. I would like to say hello to her, before she disappears, but I didn't have the guts to do so. My moral obligations were dying too slowly.

And it was hot as hell. The whole world was on fire. Well – at least the northern hemisphere. Siberia has melted. Mad Max Armageddon was on the horizon. The climate will decide, the rats will survive, and my coffee friend will laugh like he did in Noah's days.

(Meanwhile, the most powerful man in the world proudly announced to his beloved people that he – the Führer – digs coal. Cool. Cool-coal, cool-coal, tic-tac, tic-tac, BOOOOM!)

I did it. I FUCKIN' DID IT! – After drinking coffee, both

coffees, I walked over to her table. Feeling like a shaky teenager on a first date. Feeling like you're thirteen. Your second, your third date. Feeling like OH-GOD-I'M-GONNA-DIE-WITHOUT-HER! Feeling stupid, what else.

She smiled with a question in her eyes and lit a cigarette.

"Excuse me, I'm American. Do you speak English?"

(Bullshit question. It has to be. It's an alibi for a stranger to act like an idiot.)

"Don't worry, I won't bother you. Can you tell me, please, what is the best coffee brand in Trieste? There are so many of them."

(Fuck, even with an alibi, I still had a terrible stage fright.)

I saw now, she was a little older than me. Just a few years maybe. Dark beauty, a mixture of film noir coldness and post-punk fatalism. Her inner organs could be as fucked as mine too.

She smiled.

"Every coffee in Trieste is the best coffee in Trieste."

Remember this: if you get such an answer, you leave. It's impossible to get something better. She gave me everything. She gave me another smile, as if she knew the whole truth about me. As if at least one of her inner organs really is fucked.

She gave me the awareness of her existence. Much more than I asked.

I was grateful and polite as I had promised: I left, hid in the crowd and felt... something similar to happiness.

For the rest of the day I stayed at home. I could stay at home for days. And I stayed. My balcony was the only touch with the rest of the world I needed. I walked around the apartment, sticking paper notes with handwritten quotes on the furniture. This was the best job of my life.

I learned to manage my pain. It is not a regular pain, but

more like pressure or seizure. Opioids were still effective, as a medicine or a drug as well. I wasn't in a state of being high. I should reverse the phrase to be more precise: »being down« could be the right expression. »Down« to the point, without being depressed. A sticky note on the balcony wall was saying: »*Opium teaches only one thing, which is that aside from physical suffering, there is nothing real.*«

(Said a French writer I like. Have you noticed that I like a lot of French writers?)

Opioids make me high with a discrete effect: it's nothing hallucinogenic, psychedelic, or completely out of mind. Just calm and intense, it reduces your attention to a few details and makes them stronger. I have always had a very strange and intimate attitude towards drugs, but never escapist. Besides, I've never been a serious addict. For me, it was a procedure of solitude, I took drugs alone, without company.

John the Revelator was on some hard fucking drugs while writing the Apocalypse. Since then, the whole West is still on drugs, waiting for the Final Judgement. My case is no particular exception.

Fear was the reason my cardboard suitcase was only filled with books. The Gospel of John states: »*In the beginning was the Word, and the Word was with God, and the Word was God.*«

(Can an atheist deny this sentence?)

I couldn't forget that very moment I read THE sentence, I couldn't forget that smile of mine, that spontaneous smile.

When I tried to trace that absurd smile of mine, books were the first path. The path to the other side. When I found a powerful sentence, the fear lost a drop of its enormous power. It was a good path. Without words, I would have gone insane already in New York.

Leaving New York meant: I would never see my homeland again. So I will take my home with me: American writers only.

I changed my mind in a second. Home doesn't help. There is no home, or if it really exists, it is a state of mind and not a cage for your mind.

I followed the path: can you survive without Russian or French authors, without Orwell or Kundera? No, you can't – you've never really lived without reading them. Of course I will die soon, but I will die alive, that's the difference. I will become a corpse only after death, not yet alive.

(The second drop of fear vanished.)

Over the years, I became very careful about what I read. Bukowski taught me a long time ago: »*You could be sure that the worst writers had the most confidence, the least self-doubt.*«

Now I recognize the bluffing immediately. And I no longer waste my time with such a crap any more.

I don't think I'm special because of taking drugs or dying. I'm not special at all. I'm no William S. fucking Burroughs at no Chelsea fucking Hotel. I'm no fucking junkie, I'm no fucking hippie, I'm no fucking Nobel-laureate-fake-intellectual, I'm no fucking writer, I'm a fucking READER! I AM A PROFESSIONAL FUCKING READER!

My cardboard suitcase full of books is the only party ticket I have left. Ironically, the entrance fee is actually free of charge. You just walk in and you are no more.

(Same feeling as at a really good concert.)

From my past experience, I knew well the best about books: at some point in your life, you always find exactly the one that you need at that particular moment. It seems like a miracle, though it isn't: you always find the words needed to survive or – in my case – to die. Same thing.

Books are a miracle for all who seek miracles.

(Belive me: one final day, when you'll be scared shitless too, you will first see, not only hear, sentences, dialogs, lectures, sayings, poems, songs, whatever – you will keep repeating them without even knowing, yet, what the fuck happened. You'll remember, all of a sudden, a rock concert, a long time ago, you're there again, you sing the choir out loud with the band, you believe you're in heaven or hell, and – funny thing – you are, you just don't know it yet; then you grow up, you forget all that kinda bullshit, you count the money, and all of a sudden – countless tubes got stuck in your veins, doctors all around, you try to catch life, to breathe, and again, you recall that fucking song, but you can't sing, you just see the words. You see the words.)

In the morning, that song was playing in my head, a beautiful song that made me feel blue in a good way.

(No, this is neither a paradox nor a possibility of consciousness. It really felt good. You just need to transform the color. I knew: I should choose another color as soon as possible.)

After greeting the woman in black at *Pep's Caffe* another incident occurred. An incident, not a coincidence. I went to the tobacco shop. A strange black package was there – a package of unnamed tobacco. Literally without name, just »BLACK«. Nameless black tobacco. There was no other choice: I bought one.

I have no name any more. I met a woman whose name I don't know. I bought nameless tobacco.

(A joke, I thought. A killing joke. Again. Maybe my coffee friend has something to do with it.)

It was late, in the middle of the night. I transformed the color. It was black all around me. I decided to paint it gray.

I chose a tender gray color, like ashes.

## JANE'S ADDICTION: THREE DAYS

(I inform you about some events. Some days. Some time. My dramaturgical line is basically linear, but it drips in fragments. I inform you about in between time. Therefore, a script is not required. Death doesn't give a shit about time. You wanna fight death? – Erase time.)

It was hot as hell again. A strong wind blew. The storm was coming. I was looking for some weather safe place. The direction I chose was the train station. If you visit a new city but don't visit the train station, you haven't been there. Besides – the train station was in my district, it took me a few minutes to get there.

I could describe myself as a »trainspotter«. In my opinion, the two greatest British contributions in this world are: the amazing invention of the Water Closet in the first place and trainspotting in the second. Both were proof that legendary British humor exists.

(Past tense. Margaret Thatcher put it on a free market and introduced Tony Blair to the world. Not funny any more.)

This was not a train station. What I saw was a place that needs to be built. Why? – Because. Yes, there were railroad tracks. And trains. Some of them could fit into Soviet times somewhere in Eastern Europe.

(I don't get it. The Italians create all the damn clothes for all the imbeciles on Wall Street, the Italians make all the damn Ferraris and Lamborghinis and Maseratis for all the retards on

Wall Street. What the fuck happened here?)

A train to Vienna was waiting for departure. An old carriage, amazing that it has not yet been sold to India. Train to the former capital of the empire. Was it Italian cynicism that sent the worst vehicle they found up there to Vienna? Nationalism maybe?

(Nationalism certainly is Europe's greatest tragedy. The American founding fathers knew this very well. Today, one of the most powerful men in the world believes that nationalism will make America great again. Sometimes people lose touch with reality. Such condition causes historical misunderstandings. Medical treatment usually does not help.)

But then again – parallel to the railroad station there were some ruins at least two hundred meters long. Beautiful architecture, now the ruins of a large depot from the nineteenth century. Decline and fall everywhere.

I didn't get any coffee. Inside was a dystopian bar, totally sterile, politically correct, non-smoking area of course.

No soul no coffee.

I ran, the storm came. I crossed streets full of traffic, I didn't wait for the green light, I just watched the cars driving near me. When I reached *Canal Grande*, I turned around and watched the cars. And watched the cars again. I hardly saw any Italian car brands. Like America in the eighties. More precisely: since the eighties.

Detroit, I thought. This is fucking Italian Detroit! Our ruins, our decadence, foreign cars. The rain was falling down on me. I walked slowly, completely wet.

I saw the future.

As I passed Joyce's statue, I realized: I have to talk about sex now. It is my moral obligation that must be fulfilled.

(I used the adjective »moral«, knowing exactly what it means.)

Throughout history, all relevant stories represent the eternal narrative combination: sex and violence. Homer did it, Shakespeare did it and the Bible can be used as a manual instruction for all perversions possible. You want success? – Use sex, use blood, mix it, sell it and count money.

(My cardinal failure: I don't wanna use the damn formula. I'll die poor.)

Dying is violent enough, I daresay. But sex is missing. Sex and death define our world. Sex never equals pleasure, even when it's pleasant. Sex defines power, cruelty, stupidity, fear, political power, humiliation, false satisfaction, political power again and again, primitivism, misunderstanding, torture, money, damn lots of money and... if it is good – a secret, the most beautiful secret for all lovers in this world.

(These are the only two secrets in this world.)

Unfortunately my story goes beyond sex. Unless, of course, fucking with the Reaper is the ultimate erotica of a different kind. FUCK ME 'TILL I DIE!

(In my case: literally.)

Joyce's statue provoked my mind. He made me think about sex. I read the correspondence between Joyce and his beloved wife Nora Barnacle. Fuck, I was so ashamed to bother the lovers! The publisher of the couple's love letters should be hanged. The letters are »explicit«. Filthy! Dirty! Porn! Shocking! Joyce wrote it!

I would say: the letters are intimate. They should stay intimate. I'm not being conservative, just respectful. Decades after the deaths of Joyce and Nora, the letters were published in order to make some vulgar profit from the dead. The publisher should be hanged twice or simply go to the porn industry with Ron fucking Jeremy instead.

Joyce and Nora were brave and totally free. Their intimacy was almost unbelievable in the early twentieth century. It wasn't just sex they enjoyed, it was a radical social and political rebellion. Their intimacy should remain in the grave together with them only. Their imaginations were polluted. Their pride was stolen.

(Perhaps the publisher should not be hanged, but quartered.)

Joyce and Nora could no longer tolerate the ultra-conservative, religiously fanatical, nationalist Ireland. Their move to Trieste, a cosmopolitan Mediterranean port, makes sense.

In the early twentieth century, sex was still a definite taboo, although before demystification. Joyce didn't give a fuck, he busted all the myths. »*Molly Bloom's Soliloquy*« shocked the world long before Elvis Presley and The Stones.

In the early twenty-first century, only one taboo remained: death. So this is my game now.

(Remember: I still am scared shitless. I'm not bluffing.)

Quantity is the opponent. The game is stupid, the rules are made by imbeciles, the winner loses all.

Got a million? – Too bad, you need a billion!

Your dick? Ten inches? – Almost enough.

Your tits? Like oranges? – Why not melons?

The price of your car? Not even fifty thousand? – Who are you? White trash?

Your mortgage? Five hundred thousand? – You live in a dog house?

Dead at fifty? – Man or canary?

Dead at sixty? – Bad try, you moron.

Dead at seventy? – You should have prayed more and bought more guns while there was still time.

Dead at eighty? – What a shame... and life could just begin...

Dead at ninety? – Was having sex with a teenage whore at your birthday party a little too much?

Dead at a hundred? – A decent Republican.

Quantity is the only term most people understand. Having more means feeling better. Much-more-most is the only grammatical form understood by everyone. Less brains, more objects – the perfect recipe for happiness. But the problem is: people are not happy.

»*If all the rich people could be happy, capitalism would last forever.*«

(Said a... Just read the damn French writers!)

So this is my game now. It's simple: you break all the rules. Living beyond morality is the only honest ethics.

In the afternoon, after the storm, the air was clean and fresh, some kind of blue you don't see in New York City. Like Miles Davis' kind of blue. The smell of the sea everywhere, perfect time for a walk.

(I didn't forget to take my MP3 player with me. After »*Hotel California*« the risk of listening to »*Eye of the Tiger*« was all too real.)

The direction was: some interesting ruins (what else) outside the city center, which I had already seen once from a distance. I didn't know the way, I never do.

After walking for almost an hour, I found two stray cats. I was lost. Without any food for the cats.

Trieste may not be so small after all. I checked the area of both cities: New York three hundred, Trieste thirty-two square miles. Manhattan, compared to Trieste, twenty-three square miles. So it was a really long walk to meet two stray cats.

Finally I found the one and only bar across the street with all the free tables on the sidewalk. A desert. Great: Cappuccino Odyssey continues. Venue: »*Bar Buffet Alessandro*«, coffee brand Excelsior. I made an exception and only ordered a cappuccino. The same brand of coffee I drank at *James Joyce's Caffe*, but the taste was much better here.

(A friend of mine, a waitress in New York, once let me in on a secret: two people can make completely different coffee with the same coffee machine. Fuck me! – Now what about my Coffee Olympics!)

- Good evening! What happened to your espresso?
- Surprise, surprise. In this part of town?
- I have to admit, I wasn't expecting you here.
- Indeed. Still, you should order an espresso too. But you don't have to worry, I did it for both of us.
- You're visiting unholy places?
- Empty places. People took my advice to breed a little bit too overactive.
- Well... I'm childless...
- I know. Any idiot can stick his dick up someone's ass. But the trick is to stay out if you have to and feel that real tension, that slow... I told you before – people never get my basic idea. They multiply their asses to multiply more asses. There's a lot of shit going on, you know what I mean?
- Shouldn't you do something about it?
- Goddamnit! I'm fuckin' doing it! Do you think the climate crisis is a joke? Oh... did I apologize my...
- You don't have to. It's only God listening.

- You're damn right! Ever since the Tower of Babel, linguistics has been undervalued. Chaos is alwyas a linguistic problem. You know that.
- That was my suspicion, yes...
- Cut the bullshit! I have a question for you.
- No doubt. I'm listening.
- I know you've been thinking about suicide.
- Correct. I was.
- But you didn't do it.
- I did not.
- You could do it, easily, without pain. Your private drugstore has serious potential to kill not just one person but an entire rock star band.
- As I said: I did not commit suicide.
- Just let me help you, please!
- Do I have a choice...
- There is a French writer... you do like French writers, I suppose?
- I like French writers. Fuck, yes, I do.
- Now you're talking! So... will you allow me to read you an interesting passage?
- Do so, please.
- It's a short dialog, it won't take us long. And by the way – try the coffee again, it's great.

Espresso and cappuccino were on the table. He started reading. His voice changed. The color of his voice... transformed.

- *I'm not interested in suicide.*
- *Why not?*
- *Whoever kills himself is chasing the image he has created of himself. He ends his own life just to live. I don't like*

*it when a man is a fool for God.*

- You're fucking kidding me...
- I knew you'd like it. Trust me: this is important information. Especially for someone in your position. I thought it was only fair to tell you that.
- You are kidding me!
- Stop it! Living beyond morality is the only honest ethics, remember?
- I said that.
- Did you? So why is every wall in your apartment covered with notes?
- To remember, I guess.
- Are you really so afraid? If so – where did that absurd smile of yours came from?
- I'm scared shitless.
- You're not serious. Fear, you think, prevails. But still... irony has a special place in your life, right?
- Are you absolutely sure you're not the Devil?
- Please don't insult me! I last met him... let me think...
- Him? The devil?
- Yes. It was in Russia – then called the Soviet Union – almost a century ago.
- A century?
- Yes. In Moscow. I asked him for a favor.
- To do some good?
- You can put it that way if you want. I wouldn't use the word »good«. »Trade« might be a more appropriate definition.
- You were buying something?
- Selling.
- Someone's sins?

- Soul. Two souls. I sold him two souls to be exact.
- To punish them?
- Of course not. Just to let them disappear in peace.

I closed my eyes. He's not the devil, I knew that all along. When I opened my eyes, he was gone.

I returned home late, totally exhausted. My decision was clear: I will never kill myself. Notes on the wall, just notes on the wall I needed.

I took opioids first. The strange pressure on the chest was the latest innovation of my cancer cells. For a moment I thought maybe I should start drinking again. There were two perfect reasons why not. I would be – along with the opioids – stoned as hell. I saw those pathetic motherfuckers in the hospital with painkiller cocktails (mixed with bourbon) strong enough to kill an elephant. Second reason: hangover. I like mornings. Clear mornings. I chose Trieste, not Las fucking Vegas.

Notes on the wall.

I found one by a French writer I like:

»*For the first time in my life I'd started thinking about god, seriously imagining that there could be a kind of Creator of the universe observing everything I did, and my first reaction was uncomplicated, pure and simple fear.*«

(I once met the guy who wrote this. There was absolutely no fear on his face. I envied him. His face was nice and calm. Drunk too. But without fear. His thoughts are always as sharp as a blade, despite the fact that he is mostly drunk, smoking a cigarette. I believe I know what he is doing: playing a game that others don't – because he is not afraid to die.)

Hypothesis: there is a solution.

Thesis: words keep me alive. I read – I live. I read to die. Words are the bridge.

Antithesis: death means silence. No words at all. Words are death.

Synthesis: this is another motherfuckin' Catch 22 that makes no sense at all.

Bottom line: just stay scared shitless for a little longer.

## SUICIDE: FRANKIE TEARDROP

The other trainspotting day I followed the railroad and got lost. I ended up on a hill in front of the monument. A big one: total height sixty-eight meters.

»*Faro della Vittoria*« – Victory Lighthouse, built after the First World War to commemorate the transition of the city of Trieste to the Kingdom of Italy. Winged Victory Woman statue holding up a torch... sound familiar? – It is. But without wings in New York.

A comparison of the two statues reveals some historical misunderstandings. »Victory« in Trieste is at least doubtful. Italy ended the war with a disastrous defeat – the reason my great-grandfather left Trieste. He had never seen the monument and – I'm sure – he wouldn't give a shit about it. He picked the real winners.

»Liberty« in New York is a cynicism of a different kind: it is a false prophecy of the future, not of the past, as in Trieste.

Both examples prove to us that myths and irony are incompatible. Power has no sense of humor. Only the court jester can use it.

There was a restaurant nearby: »*Trattoria Al Faro*«. At nine a.m. no food had been served yet. The outside terrace was empty, I was the only guest. Employees were arranging the restaurant premises but one of them brought me coffee after I introduced myself as an American. You don't say NO to a superpower.

Cappuccino Odyssey, next stop: posh restaurant, Bristot coffee brand. Espresso & cappuccino.

(I ordered both because I wasn't in the mood for an unexpected visitor to remind me I forgot my espresso.)

The Italian Renaissance took place here from the forteenth to the seventeenth century. It changed the world dramatically.

America should be the new renaissance. At the very beginnings, we were. Our Constitution was a masterpiece of American Enlightenment. We were faster than the French. The Bolsheviks came far behind us and were the first to screw up.

The USA introduced the idea, all the people will rule.

(»People« can only be white people of Anglo-Saxon origin and Protestant faith. Animals can be painted as desired.)

The French Revolution introduced the idea that all men are equal.

(Ask Napoleon.)

The Bolsheviks introduced the idea that all workers would rule.

(They did. In gulags.)

After the collapse of communism, we praise our final victory like the Italians praise their lighthouse. To prove my hypothesis about historical misunderstandings, I argue that we never defeated communism. The Communists – this time the Chinese – are beating us. Again, I have to be more specific: not beating, but eating us.

(They eat everything, everyone knows that.)

America is scared shitless. The empire is falling apart. We believe that only force, brute force, can ensure our survival. This is an act of panic. Now we will encounter all the worst mistakes that we tried to avoid in the past. That's the difference between me and my country: the USA will commit suicide, I won't.

The American renaissance dates back to the Dark Ages; our way goes backwards.

Brutal power is an infantile method. We have certainly dominated this world, but by no means with nuclear missiles – our soft power has made us the greatest country in the world. We won with Marlon Brando, with ass-shaking Elvis Presley, with blue denim.

(We never forced anyone to wear jeans. The world was happy to do it themselves. Fuck the facts.)

Instead of a renaissance, we now have conspiracy theories. Instead of enlightenment, we count flying pigs and evil witches. We are »*lost in a Roman wilderness of pain, and all the children are insane*«.

The Roman Empire ruled the world from here two thousand years ago. In the end it was destroyed by the Christians. Of course, also with the sword of the barbarians, but above all, the empire could no longer fight the idea. Lack of ideas meant defeat. The motivation was gone, the wilderness of pain was already shining on the horizon: Attila the Hun was the rising star. We should never underestimate the fall of empires: the whole world sinks with them.

When exactly did I formally realize that America is fucked? – It was easy: suddenly our films became great again. The Berlin Wall is falling to pieces. Deng Xiaoping in China no longer gives a fuck about the color of a cat – as long as that damn cat catches mice. Russia is on a unique highway to hell with notoriously drunk president and plutonium for sale at the fish market. Globalization took the form of T-Rex overnight.

But we... started producing impressive movies and TV shows.

Previously, the Oscar-winning Rocky had the same status as Michelangelo's David in Florence. Miami Vice in the eighties can be seen from Martin Heidegger's point of view as the purest »DA-SEIN«, even though the negro character should be killed to achieve divine perfection. Ronald Reagan, an actor, not coincidentally, was president at the time; John Rambo was in charge of foreign affairs; Chuck Norris helped with some of the trickier situations, including low taxes and corporate freedom.

However, pretty soon Rambo urgently needed plastic surgery and Chuck Norris became No. one joke all around the flat globe.

Movies made America great again. It was an unexpected shock. After decades of political and religious politeness, after decades of lies, suddenly almost everything I saw on the screen was real, it was true. Everyone knew that. Everyone saw what I saw. Everyone was telling the truth: Detroit is fucked, we drive some carlike things with some weird new names like KIA. What goes around, comes around. We didn't believe it. We hoped like Chuck Norris that the Earth would be finally flat after all. But the cinema didn't lie any more. The film succeeded in selling the truth. If you can sell the truth, you have solid proof that the world is fucked, seriously fucked. Audiences accepted the message because myth was not a solid currency to pay the bills. Although Rambo survived several plastic surgeries, he could no longer maintain the myth. Louis XIV, the Sun King of France, never washed his entire life, a legend tells. There is a save assumption that he stank like a motherfucker.

(He left behind... the Palace of Versailles, a magnificent building without a single toilet. Now we can understand why

British civilization later won the imperial race – the Brits did not forget toilets.)

We are now losing our empire because we no longer believe in our values.

(Have we ever, really? Chuck Berry or Little Richard succeeded, but not because America was so democratic or tolerant. They succeeded because they could sell race music to a white audience. It happened for profit. Selling records was just business as usual. Black money doesn't stink either.)

We were strong, we became a superpower as long as we believed in at least a little liberty and a drop of justice. Now greed is the only idea we have left. Selfishness is the only guide. Our last idea was deregulation, but we didn't deregulate the economy, we deregulated society as such. Without regulation, we have opened Pandora's box of chaos. All the children became insane, indeed. Our future is vulgarity and – in the words of Hunter S. Thompson – primitivism: »*All political power comes from the barrel of either guns, pussy, or opium pipes, and people seem to like it that way.*«

Now we are full of shit. And you can't shit the shiter. We don't need enemies, we are capable of exterminating ourselves.

(By the way: if we had fought at Stalingrad, the Germans would have crushed us in a week. We don't possess what the Russians have: imagination. We buy imagination, just like everything else. Imagination is a terrifying weapon. And you can't buy it on the free market.)

I forgot about both statues, victory, liberty, misunderstandings, lies, America, Russia, China, chaos, power, more lies. I forgot about the so-called serious topics, ran home, made another coffee (at home it's Illy), took drugs and looked for another note on the wall.

»*I think it's important to live in a nice country rather than a powerfull one. Power makes everybody crazy.*«

(No fuckin' French writer said that. On the contrary – he was an American. The one who survived the bombing of Dresden in 1945. The guy who saw hell with his naked eyes. And came back from hell alive. And couldn't stop laughing...)

Is Italy a nice country? – I have no fucking idea. I don't know Italy. And I seriously suspect: Italy doesn't even know Trieste at all. Geographically and politically, Trieste hardly belongs to Italy. Perhaps Trieste is the only non-Italian Italian city.

(Is Italy a powerfull country? – Well... if there are some nuclear missiles here, they can only be American. Spaghetti makes it hard to kill enemies. And I saw old posters for Bruce Springsteen and Patti Smith concerts on billboards. Maybe pasta and rock'n'roll can prove that Italy is a nice country rather than a powerful one. My great-grandfather would disagree.)

In the afternoon, the wind embraced the city. I knew nothing about the wind in Trieste or the nickname »windy city«. I thought Chicago was the only one. It's not. Trieste is famous for the wind »Bora« in the north direction from the mountains to the Gulf of Trieste. This can be a very strong and cold wind, especially in winter.

The wind warned us: the fall is coming. My time was running out, but I planned to make it through the fall and into the winter.

(I went to the doctor the day before. He said I was still too alive to take morphine. I felt sorry for the guy: according to the concept of modern Western medicine, I was dying too slowly. Anyway – I only took my prescriptions. He suggested taking more vitamins instead of opioids. I explained that the next

Olympics was not my primary goal, and I had no plans to go vegan. The doctors hate me, I leave them no other choice.)

The »*G-bar*« was placed on the square with the church. Holy trinity: square-church-café as usual. The waitress came quickly and I did something I had never done before: I asked what brand of coffee they were serving.

The girl was pissed in a second and explained what a total idiot her boss was. Now, instead of Illy, they offer Hausbrandt. And it stinks, her boss, his mother is a big fan of garlic and the boss's wife has no right to share any comments about her mother-in-law and her kitchen. A lot of intimate information for a stranger she was seeing for the first time in her life.

(I assumed the wife didn't even have a license to cook.)

Hausbrandt was fine, the waitress was fine, but the wind got stronger, smoking was impossible. On the other side of the church it was calm, the church stopped the wind.

Cappuccino Odyssey sped up a bit with the wind.

I found the next two cafés. Neighbors. The first was »*Bar Nico*«. Can you ignore a bar named *Nico*? – You can't.

(I could never forget the story of the real Nico. After being a huge addict all her life, she finally got clean. And died shortly after while riding her bike. She was forty-nine years old. The irony killed her. It was a punishment for giving up drugs. I won't give up drugs, but I will die at the same age. Irony of a different kind.)

I sat down, got a portion of espresso + cappuccino, but the brand of coffee was Dersut, from the bar next to *Nico*. *Nico* had Excelsior. Dersut came from »*Bar Armagnac*«. It was a mess. Who charges what? Nobody cared. No one was upset.

The simplicity of this world is brutal. That is its only beauty.

There was a poster on the *Nico's* front door. Unfortunately, it was Uncle Sam with the following advise:
HEY TU
AIUTACI A TENERE
PULITO IL RIONE!
I didn't know what it meant. I still don't. Get a translation if you want. It's a kind of communication game.

I could see the port from my *Nico*-position at the table. Everywhere you go in Trieste, you see the port. It is a huge port that takes up half of the city. We can only imagine how important it was at its peak, deep back in the nineteenth century. Somehow I've already tried to find access to countless docks, but it is forbidden. Even for a superpower.

(I engage in another forbidden activity: every evening I swim on the main promenade, including Borgo Teresiano. I swim in the Canal Grande, at its very beginning, where it touches the open sea. I don't give a fuck and nobody gives a shit. So maybe Italy or at least Trieste is a nice place.)

Ports are all we have left in the West. Ports and trucks. Logistics. We care a lot about someone else's crap. This makes us garbage people. We no longer control anything except the arrival-departure schedule.

(I often see »Holland America Line« cruise ships here. My type. They usually end their trip in Venice. I'm curious about Venice. There must be something about Venice. The most magical place in the world, they say. I wonder why it was a German who wrote the famous novel »*Death in Venice*«.)

Next to *Nico* was a second-hand shop. I jumped in. All kinds of vintage trash. But a small relief of the Virgin Mary caught my attention – I bought it immediately. Protestant America doesn't care about the apparently intact Virgin Mary, but Catholics are crazy about her. They don't seem to care about God, as the Holy Virgin is a better tool for increasing profits. That's probably true. Women's bodies are easier to sell. For example, prostitution mostly sells women's bodies. I believe you noticed that.

The relief was fascinating. Mary with golden hair wears a nobel blue scarf. Her lip-flip-lips are painted with red lipstick. Eyebrows like Marlene Dietrich in »*The Blue Angel*«. Despite her half-closed eyes, she is cautiously looking down somewhere. A professional mathematician would prove that her gaze would stop exactly in the middle of the person's body, probably a male person, standing in front of her. You don't see that kind of look in the Protestant world.

I like Catholics, I admire Catholics. They are the only honest Christians. Of course, they have their own rules and commitments, but they don't even pretend to respect them. The Catholic world is therefore easy to understand. First you check the official moral obligations. Second – you turn them upside down. You are now entering Catholic reality. What you find is the Pope with a big smile.

The Protestant environment is more complex, the hypocrisy more sublime and disgusting. Basically, pastors lie in the same way as Catholic priests lie. The essential difference is: pastors believe their own lies. And they never laugh. They are just calling for the next crusade without a smile on their faces.

Late evening.

I was staring at the photo on the internet. The war in Syria. A guy stands in front of his house, which was totally destroyed after the bombing.

A few days after the death of Diego Maradona, the god of football. Real football, not American football. Americans play

FOOTball with their hands.

So what does the guy in Syria do now? Is he fixing his house? He runs? He fights? – No. He painted a mural, a portrait of his dead idol on the wall. The only wall of the house remained and still standing.

It ain't war that matters, it's the football player – he provides the real spectacle, the bombs do not.

I have never seen an image that was more explicit and meaningful. It explains everything essential – political and emotional – related to human society and intimacy as well: everything is irrational. The meaning is irrational. We are all irrational: we can only choose our own kind of insanity.

(This is not a paradox, this is – obviously – the possibility of irrational consciousness. There are no meanings. No logic. There is fear. And spectacle as a tool to mask fear. Fiction wins, always.)

Now I know how this world works. What should I do next? I won't paint any murals, certainly not. I'm not a painter, I'm a reader. Shall I prepare my last words? My own words or the words of some fuckin' French writer?

I'm American. I choose my own, American insanity. I remember so well the very best farewell sentence ever, namely – Johnny Cash's last words are rumored to be:

»I hear the train a-comin.«

(I can steal that. And I will. I must not be so scared shitless to forget it.)

# THE STOOGES: WE WILL FALL

*»Ideas improve. The meaning of words participates in the improvement. Plagiarism is necessary. Progress implies it. It embraces an author's phrase, makes use of his expressions, erases a false idea, and replaces it with the right idea.«*
Guy Debord

I did it. I FUCKIN' DID IT! – I took a trip to Venice.

**Your decision to travel to Venice is at least bizarre. Can you argue with that?**

- I agree. It was neither my plan nor an impulsive idea. Maybe I was just too high. Last night I got some unexpected cocaine at the bar.

**What was the name of the bar?**

- I won't tell.

**That sounds suspicious. You always tell the name because of your Cappuccino Odyssey research.**

- I didn't drink coffee, so the name of the bar doesn't count.

**What did you drink?**

- Tonic water. The bartender was really nice to me. I strongly assume he's gay.

**He sold you cocaine?**

- He gave me cocaine for free, but I had to promise him that I would visit Venice. He insisted. According to my oath, he gave me cocaine. To have a nice trip, he said.

**Are you homosexual?**

- I have never noticed such behavior on behalf of my person.

**Do you really believe that you visited Venice on the advice of a bartender?**

- Absolutely not. I wanted to discover why it was a German writer who wrote »*Death in Venice*«.

**Which transport did you use?**

- Train.

**Can you explain your obsession with trains? It seems pathetic.**

- There is a decadent French writer who describes two nineteenth century locomotives in a fascinatingly erotic way...

**Cut off that endless French crap! You are boring. When did you leave Trieste?**

- I woke up at six a.m. The train was scheduled to depart at eight sixteen a.m.

**What happened in between?**

- I took a shower...

**Stop! Why did you decide to take a trip? How did you know when the train left the station?**

- I took my opioids along with some cocaine. Maybe the mixture was kinda explosive. So I went. And of course I didn't know when the train would leave. Eventually it turned out that the train to Venice runs every hour.

**Was the train a Soviet type?**

- Well, I don't think so...

**Have you ever seen a Soviet train in your life?**

- No, I have not. But I really...

**You're full of bullshit. What happened on the train first?**

- First, I got a great window seat. Then I went to the

toilet...

**Toilet? What for?**

- I was so happy with my seat that I went to the toilet to get some more cocaine. To celebrate in a way...

**You could sniff some in the car. With discretion. Why in the toilet?**

- I use a needle. Intravenous is more effective.

**You're a sick fuck! What's next?**

- Some gang... maybe Gypsies... surrounded me in the car. They were very loud.

**So your celebration was in vain. Gypsies? You sure?**

- Well... maybe they weren't Gypsies, but Italians from the deep south of Italy ...

**Deep south? Trieste is located in the north-east of Italy. North-east as far as it goes. Your story sucks. Do you have you at least one argument for your guess?**

- During their conversation, I recognized the word »*Napoli*« several times.

**You don't speak or understand Italian, especially not dialects. If one of the »Gypsies« said »Kentucky Fried Chicken«, would you hear it quite differently than »Napoli«?**

- Probably not.

**What did the landscape look like?**

- Awful. Incredibly boring. I saw the Victory Lighthouse on the hill for the first time since the day I got lost. Then the train went inland, away from the sea, nothing to see.

**Nothing, absolutely nothing to remember?**

- We passed a territory called California. It doesn't look like California, but it says everything about the world we live in.

**Oh... sure – your American Empire theory?**
- About the collapse of the American Empire, yes.

**You are not a patriot. Do you hate your homeland so much?**
- I protest! I really love my country, honestly! It hurts to watch it fall apart.

**Are you sure there is nothing left but the downfall of the USA?**
- As sure as I am about my cancer.

**When will you die?**
- I hope in the spring. A few more months to go.

**How long did the trip to Venice take?**
- Two hours, five minutes.

**How many times have you used the toilet?**
- Four times. About every thirty minutes.

**To do what?**
- I actually did piss once.

**Were you excited? About Venice?**
- Not at all. I knew from the very beginning that the trip was a failure.

**And you went on a trip anyway? Why?**
- I have to practice. I wanna fail better.

**You really are a sick fuck. When did you arrive in Venice?**
- At ten twenty-six a.m. with a slight delay.

**What did you notice first?**
- The Germans. Most of the people on the streets were Germans. The first drink on the menu of every restaurant was »Spritz«.

**Do you know what the word »Spritz« means?**
- No. But it sounds German.

**Did you walk? Where?**
- I remember walking across the Rialto Bridge.

**Across the Grand Canal? What were you thinking at that moment?**
- I got the answer to why »*Death in Venice*« was written by a German.

**Did you? Explain!**
- Melancholy. The Germans are said to be the most warlike nation in the world. Up there in Germany, everything is flat, boring, the climate sucks. You become nuts, melancholy makes you kill people. In your free time you come down here for a while. Melancholy overtakes you again: eventually you like the place, but no one threatens to kill you. So you need another tragedy, like a sad love story. The more warlike you are, the more sentimental you become.

**Could you answer diplomatically?**
- I don't want to cause an international incident. Besides, It wasn't me who described the Germans as the most warlike nation in the world. It's Kurt Vonnegut's fault – he did it after visiting the Octoberfest in Munich.

**Was there a lot of pigeon shit?**
- In Munich?

**You're not funny. Were there countless pigeons in Venice?**
- I saw exactly four pigeons. They seemed too exhausted to shit around.

**What about the smell?**
- Nothing special. No dead rats in the water.

**Are you sure you've been to Venice?**
- Absolutely. I still keep the train ticket as proof. And a photo of four exhausted pigeons.

**What impressed you the most?**
- I couldn't find a single trash can and no public bench to sit on for a while.

**Tell us more about the Doge's Palace!**
- More.

**Not only are you full of shit, but you're also extremely cynical. The New York Times describes Venice as »the most beautiful city built by man«. Did you know that?**
- The New York Times described the 2003 US invasion on Iraq as a peaceful mission to deliver flowers and butterflies to the desert around Baghdad. Did you know that?

**Is there anything you like about Venice at all?**
- Giacomo Casanova.

**The gigolo?**
- The writer. A brilliant Venetian writer. He fucked a lot of women, but he wasn't a male prostitute.

**Would you live in Venice?**
- I'd rather live with penguins in Antarctica.

**You often mention penguins. Do you like birds?**
- I feel sorry for them. Evolution has treated this species extremely cruelly: birds just eat and shit permanently without knowing why. They all seem exhausted and depressed to me. I believe they deserve some existential empathy.

**Could your surprising empathy also flow in the gondolas of Venice?**
- Sink, not flow.

**Did you buy any souvenirs?**
- Yes. Train ticket back to Trieste.

**You're being sarcastic again. Don't you think traveling can improve your knowledge?**
- Only complete idiots believe that. Traveling is just

expensive and doesn't improve anything. If traveling gave you any knowledge, the smartest man on the planet would be the one with the biggest yacht. I dare to doubt that.
**When did you return?**
- The train left Venice at one thirty-nine p.m.

**Excuse me! You said you arrived in Venice at ten twenty-six, which means you only stayed in Venice for two hours and thirteen minutes?**
- Exactly.

**Do you realize that people from all over the world travel the world just to see Venice, if they are lucky enough to see Venice at all in their lifetime?**
- Well... people are strange.

**You are a disgrace to humanity! Are you aware of this too?**
- I guess so. But you don't have to worry, I promise. I will die soon, besides I have not shared my genetic potential with any other being. The damage done cannot be so terrible.

The train was full. No airflow. No air conditioning. No chance to open the window. And finally – all the toilets were closed. Nevermind I've never seen a Soviet train – I can't imagine the Central Committee not allowing citizens to at least urinate.

(And drink vodka in public without hiding.)

This was the first time I left Trieste. And used transport. I knew it would never happen again. La mia anima è a Trieste. Thinking about Trieste was thinking about home. A home like I've never felt in New York. Surrounded by tourists from all over the world, I could start screaming. To scream out they should all go fuck themselves along with the damn Venice. To tell the world how magical Trieste really is, not Venice – not

that kitschy Mediterranean Disneyland.
- Excuse me, can I sit here?
My bag was on the opposite window seat. I took it in my lap.
- Yeah, sure. Please.
- I believe that your disappointment with Venice is sincere.
- Goddamn! I didn't recognize you... I'm sorry!
- Don't be.
- It's because of your beret...
- A dear present. I got it a long time ago.
- A very elegant gray beret, I must say. Let me guess... nearly a hundred years old?
- Please stop! I asked you something else.
- About disappointment? It may not be the right word. Anger would be an appropriate term, I think.
- I disagree. We will discuss it. But first – this is the last car of the train.
- So?
- Go straight to the end. There is a small hidden seat that is only used by train employees. Passengers don't see it. And a small window. I opened it for you. I know you need both.
- Why are you doing this?
- I told you before: I'd like to help.
- In exchange for...?
- For the right answer, of course. Now go! No one will notice. I will watch. If the conductor comes, I'll whistle.
- Your gray beret... I think I know...
- Don't forget your needle and cigarette. Go! You owe me an answer.

I went. The seat was there. The window was open. I

enjoyed it two, maybe three minutes, nothing more. And... I was sure about the beret: an old, noble, timeless beret. It must once have belonged to a »*man of wealth and taste*« ...
- Thank you!
- You're back quickly.
- I cannot piss through the window. But I accomplished all the rest.
- You did?
- You mean the answer? I did it too. It's too obvious.
- Listening.
- This is not a disappointment. It is absurd.
- You are a good student. Venice is not about beauty or gondolas or stinking water or St. Mark's Basilica.
- I know.
- Venice is not about Venice at all.
- I know that too. It's about perception that has nothing to do with the object. Just like your beret.
- I'm glad my beret was able to help. I will leave you now.
- I understand. Thank you!
- You understand... this is an impressive example of self-confidence. Something new about you, indeed. Can I ask you one more question before I go?
- Please.
- Did you buy a souvenir in Venice?
- You're kidding me! Again.
- I'm dead serious. Please don't insult me!
- I apologize, I didn't mean to...
- Did you buy a souvenir?
- Well... no... I don't have any fuckin' souvenir! And excuse my language...

- Fuck language! You've seen hundreds of shops, correct?
- I have. Along with hundreds of Germans buying carnival masks.
- Exactly!
- Sorry, I'm not following this...
- Maybe you're not as good a student as I thought. Have you seen the masks? Venetian carnival masks? Aren't they beautiful? If, of course, you forget about perception, which has nothing to do with the object.
- We could say that, yes...
- You should buy one.
- A mask? Which mask?
- The Death mask. You need one.

For a moment I lost my breathe. Just for a moment and then I smiled. It came out of nothing again, that absurd smile of mine.
- I do?
- Of course. Or have you lost your sense of irony? Or do you plan to stay scared shitless to the very end?
- Maybe I'm a really bad student.
- Try harder. And have coffee in Trieste. I know you couldn't drink it in Venice.
- It would be a blasphemy.
- Oh... now it's my duty to support your opinion! Anyway – don't forget the espresso. You can pretend it's for me.
- I will.

At two forty-eight p.m. I arrived back to Trieste. First I blessed the station with a lot of holy water from my dick. I was entitled to such baptism.

(I literally blessed the station. My coffee friend didn't unlock the toilet on the train. I guess he was punishing me for not being a perfect student.)

I walked to »*Piazza Oberdan*« with my eyes almost closed. But even though my eyes were closed, I was safe, the city took care of me. I stopped at the tram station. Former tram station, today the tram does not run. Only the rails remained. I sympathized with those missing trams.

»*Bar Tivoli*« was the closest. Coffee brand: Julius Meinl. Bar owner: Chen Jianfeng. The USA and the UK will never come back. Instead, the Chinese are already here.

Salvation from Venice (and New York) convinced me, for good: yes, I will die here in Trieste. The universe ends here.

Unfortunately, we have to continue talking about empires. The reason for this is simple: I wanted to take a leak. Usually, such a biological need can be resolved without complications, unless if you suffer from a bizarre mental condition. But in this case it was not a psychological deviation. The toilet was there. The door was open. So far, the world has seemed predictable.

The first surprise was: there were no separate rooms for ladies and gentleman. Borrowing Martin Heidegger's terminology again, we could say that »WC-DA-SEIN« existed in the form of a single room. An unexpected phenomenon. And in that room was this... device.

I was forced to believe that this... device... somehow has its own ontological meaning.

This... device... was some sort of ceramic hole in the ground. A hole and a place for your feet. It was possible for a man to take a leak there, I must admit, but any other more sophisticated action due to the needs of the human body would certainly become a gymnastic miracle, especially for women.

I thought that perhaps such a... device... could be the result of the Chinese ontological perception of the world. Perhaps the Chinese have never read Martin Heidegger.

(If so, they are some lucky bastards.)

And there was also one sink. I just couldn't get water from the pipe. Fortunately, fate is sometimes merciful. Instructions in English were written on the wall: »To wash your hands, press the water pedal under the sink.«

So I did. And I washed my hands.

The lesson of this fable is: we know now for sure why the British Empire once became world superpower. This did not happen because of the industrial revolution in Great Britain; it was not technological progress; it is the water closet. The Brits have solved humanity's basic problem: how to get rid of unnecessary materials in a decent way. And to even have the opportunity to think in peace while completing this delicate process.

I didn't look for any suitable quote on my walls before I went to sleep. I was just wondering how impossible it is to separate the intimate essence from the social and political environment.

Death is politics. The biggest nonsense of all. The cardinal absurd.

# ROBERT JOHNSON: COME ON IN MY KITCHEN

Early in the morning I was surprised by an unexpected trouble. I was making coffee, or at least trying to, when suddenly I could no longer feel the right side of my body. My leg vanished, the spoon fell from my hand. Pins and needles all over, including the right side of my face. For all I know, this could be a sign of a stroke. At first I panicked, then I got angry – a man with terminal cancer deserves a longer, more painful death, not this vulgar rush without even a chance to wash, shave and put on a nice suit.

I took a shot of cocaine immediately. I knew, we all know what can harm us. And we keep doing it, regardless of whether our action will kill us or not. It is the only way to face possible death. This is the only way to die, to accept death. Otherwise, we eat and shit like exhausted Venetian pigeons and end up not dying but disappearing. Honestly, most people just eat and shit.

(I met a very old guy in Brooklyn who always sat on a bench in front of his store, smoked about four packs of cigarettes a day and drank a bottle of Wild Turkey. »*I live long,*« he explained to me, »*because I watch someone else die instead of me. It doesn't have to be human, it can be an animal or a tree. But it has to be an obvious sacrifice, I have to see that. I have to be careful, I respect these deaths. I remember them all. I take photos and write down the circumstances of their death in my notebook. Every death gives me a little more life. But that doesn't mean I'm a parasite. I only pay attention* to creatures that no one has ever noticed. They thank me for that. It's about mutual gratitude. I always bury animals that died for me: dogs, spiders, bats. I would gladly do the same with people, but in that case the authorities would put me in an asylum like an old lunatic. In fact, I'm just trying to be kind. One day I too will die for someone else. I will pass my secret on to someone who understands.«)

When invented in the nineteenth century, cocaine was used as a local anesthetic. Sigmund Freud used it as a narcotic for years. I followed his majestic example of a drug fiend.

I kind of took a shower sitting down. I prepared to be clean, just in case. I put on a nice gray suit.

I wanted out as soon as possible. I could barely walk, so I stopped nearby at »*Caffe Eppinger*«. First, I was offered Illy coffee, which was great. Second, I was forced to listen to a jazzy cover version of Madonna's »*Material Girl*«. Not the last song you wanna hear before you drop dead.

It was a fresh morning, and Bora was blowing through the streets. I didn't mind, I felt better. But I knew Bora would definitely hit really hard in the winter.

Needles and pins in my body lost a bit of power. I went to the toilet to continue Freud's anti-anxiety method.

(Nice, clean toilet without any surprises or... devices. Too bad I didn't use it for its basic purpose.)

Madonna's song encouraged me to describe a brief history of the USA. Both coffees were great, the task was a piece of cake, but I had to wait until the so-called stroke killed me or I could feel my body symmetrical again. Some time lost to political economy was acceptable. It was my American moral obligation to express my viewes on the country I come from and where I have lived all my life. About the country that defines me: The United States of America.

Hypothesis 1 (espresso): economic liberalism created this country.

Hypothesis 2 (cappuccino): economic liberalism will destroy this country.

Argument 1: you steal land and resources, wipe out previous owners, invent slavery and the free market. You compete with the rest of the world with your products. Your alibi is freedom. Freedom to steal and kill. Your primitive-original accumulation of capital is astonishing. You win. Greed is good.

Argument 2: you move your production to China. You invent cheap human resources and present them with a free market. You eliminate your domestic American workers. You compete with the rest of the world with your products. Your profits increase dramatically. Your alibi is freedom. Greed is good.

Mistake 1: your success is not due to genius, but to violence.

Mistake 2: China invents slavery, eliminates human rights, embraces the free market, steals your technology, and competes with the rest of the world with its own cheaper products. The Chinese alibi is freedom. Freedom to steal and kill. China's success is due not to genius, but to violence. Now you're fucked. Your holy greed is killing you. You're pissed. You print enormous amount of worthless papers – dollars, otherwise you can no longer survive. You count your nuclear missiles: you need them to protect your worthless papers. IN GOD WE TRUST, you say.

Suddenly I felt something on my back. It was not wind, but like wind. It was him. I learned to feel his presence. He didn't

order coffee, he didn't say good morning, he started asking me questions.
- Why do you think you're scared?
- Because I am. I'm scared shitless.
- You're not. You learned.
- Learn? Learn what?
- You have learned fear. You are not afraid. You're on the other side already.
- I'm dead?
- No. You have reached immortality. You don't want it, you despise it. But you cannot beat the irony. You talk to me, for example.
- So what?
- Either you're insane or you've lost your fear.
- I choose to be insane.
- But you're not.
- I don't believe you. I am afraid. I'm scared shitless.
- No, you're not. Fear is far behind you.
- You're fucking kidding me. Again and again.
- Have you just had a stroke?
- I don't know.
- Wrong answer. Give me the right one.
- I don't fucking care whether it was a stroke or not.
- Correct.
- So?
- You don't care. You washed, shaved, put on a nice suit. People don't do things like that out of fear. They cry, call their mother and shit their pants.
- What color is fear?
- Usually blue.
- Blue was my favorite color a long time ago. Now I

can't stand it. I prefer...
- ... gray.
- Yes. Gray. Just like your beret...
- Drink two more coffees. And don't worry – it wasn't a stroke.
- No?
- No, you fucking asshole! Cocaine was invented as a local anesthetic, remember?
- Oh, shit... I temporarily paralyzed myself?
- See you soon! Just stick to gray.

The waiter brought me another espresso and cappuccino. He was asking me (or perhaps explaining?) something in some Slavic language. Motherfucker obviously didn't recognize me as a foreigner. On the contrary – he saw me as a member of his tribe. Great. I have officially become a native »Triestino«.

I had to finish my brief history of the USA. To leave it all behind. It wasn't much more to say.

Political economy makes absolutely no sense. Economic concepts are always ideological concepts. America has created the biggest economic nonsense of all time: the richest world in history, with no possibility for the majority to live decently without dept. The method for doing this is called »trickle-down«.

(A New Zealand member of parliament has described exactly what America's »trickle-down« really means: the rich pissing down on the poor.)

America needs permanent war. War makes sense. First: war keeps social relations – patriotism, nationalism – strong. Second, and even more important: war ensures continued production. The only production left. Detroit is dead.

The USA of the twenty-first century is a banana republic

with an alpha male gorilla in charge.

(Some deep, honest apologies to the actual gorillas are absolutely necessary.) Throughout two centuries of American history, millions of hard working slaves (not just blacks) died while looking at the magnificent buildings they built. America they built. A sea of desire destroyed by their own masters, the masters of collective ignorance, selfishness and greed.

It all started with a Bible and a gun. It all started with genocide. And it will all end with it. This doesn't mean white versus black. It can mean white versus yellow. And most likely white against white. The last genocide will be that of the white race: pure cannibalism. Exorcism. The KKK will win the presidential election.

After two hundred and fifty years of history, the USA will now repeat all the European mistakes that this country has successfully avoided from the very beginning. As the saying goes, mistakes are common. Normal. Human. We have the right to make mistakes. We will improve. We will approach wisdom. The USA is proof that the saying goes completely wrong. It's pure bullshit. There are no mistakes. Mistakes only show stupidity. This is why religion is so important in America: it corrects mistakes. To deny mistakes. IN GOD WE TRUST.

(Unfortunately, god is on permanent vacation. He doesn't give a fuck about stupidity. I know him well enough to say that. God is not America's ally. He is no one's ally. He can help, but only to those who listen, not to those who demand.)

I felt good. I felt like native Triestino. I felt my body again. Now I was ready – for the first time – to visit the central café in Trieste: »*Caffè degli Specchi*« in *Piazza Unita*. I went there, it was close. Bora helped me with some push in the back. I was laughing: my coffee friend was right as always. I do not fear, I chose fear. I chose to play a game that other people don't because they are afraid to die. And I will lose because I have to. And I can shit my pants from laughing, not from fear.

Now I finally knew where that absurd smile of mine came from, where it was born: on the other side.

*Caffè degli Specchi* was full as always, but I got a free table. Of course, this was a fancy place for tourists. I couldn't care less: I wasn't one of them, I was a fucking dead man.

I got my fancy tray with coffee (brand: Segafredo), water, a small glass of hot chocolate and a cookie.

It was time to finish the brief history of the USA. I had a tiny book with me. The title of the book was »Truth about Los Angeles«, written in 1927 by the American author Louis Adamic. Never heard of this guy, found his name recommended in Philip Roth's notes. In his book, Adamic quotes a newspaper article:

### VIVE LA GUILLOTINE

*Recent despatches are full of the righteous wrath of man. A Stamboul hodja and some forty of his partisans have been condemned to death by hanging for opposing the Turkish Kemal Pasha in his decree replacing the fez with the hard-boiled derby.*

*In our own enlightened land, one, prominent in official circles, calls loudly for the whipping post as fit punishment for the defamer of our first president.*

*I believe in this. I have always held that no punishment was too severe for one who entertained opinions contrary to mine.*

*We – that is, those who accord with my views – must stand*

shoulder to shoulder and get more laws passed. Laws that are more stringent, more exacting. Punishment in the past has been too lenient.

To call a man a traitor to his country – a poltroon – a destroyer of the Constitution – when his views are diametrically opposed to my views – may answer in some circles, but I stand for the rack and thumbscrew.
*The man who thinks for himself must go!*
*Down with him!*
*If not down with him, fetch a rope and – up with him!*
*Thank God, we live in a free country!*

Adamic was an immigrant and a proud American in the first half of the twentieth century. He emigrated to the USA at the age of fifteen. His analyzes of American society are brilliant. Only an immigrant can keep his distance and at the same time be deeply and honestly loyal to his country. Immigrants built this country, brought innovation and made America great.

A century later, when Adamic wrote his book, »la guillotine« shines on the horizon like never before. His prophecies, his fears were justified.

(That's why he was killed at his home in New Jersey in 1951. No one knows who killed him.)

In the end, of course, China will win. In 2011, the Communist Party introduced a magnificent new statue in Tiananmen Square in downtown Beijing. It wasn't a statue of Mao or Deng or any other Communist jerk.

It was Confucius. At that moment I knew for sure: they will conquer the world because they believe, they truly believe. Their respect for tradition, their belief ain't no fake. Our faith is a lie, we don't keep the Ten Commandments, never have. We only use them as an alibi for killing, stealing and cheating.

China's vulgar economy will winn. But like the Soviets before them, the Chinese also lack soft power. They will never sell Confucius to the rest of the world like we sold blue denim and rock'n'roll.

America's basic idea was revolutionary: we were ready to welcome and accept anyone. No other country in history has ever done this. It was a great, brave attempt. Now, in the twenty-first century, the land of the free and home of the brave is becoming a nightmare. We fucked it all up. Our retribution begins. It will be pure horror of poverty and violence.

»*The real revolution is retreat. The point is, you're not involved. Instead of passive resistance, active desertion must be chosen today.*«

(Said a French writer, full of cocaine and alcohol. I like and admire this bastard for many reasons, including his love for America. His ability to see what America really is. Most Americans would probably hate him.)

I stood in the middle of *Piazza Unita* and watched the blue of the sea. A kind of blue you don't see in New York.

I was left alone with my personal revolution only. Revolutions are often associated with the color red. Revolutions devour their own children.

I chose my revolution to be gray. I will leave no child behind.

## NEUROSIS: BRIDGES

»*Be careful with quotations, you can damn anything.*«
André Malraux

A beautiful autumn day. Probably one of the last. My last one. Bora stopped for a while. When it comes back, I start counting days.

I was sitting in front of James Joyce's apartment in Trieste. *Via Donato Bramante four*, second floor, San Vito district, not downtown, about twenty minutes away from my *Borgo Teresiano*.

(Joyce lived with Nora in several different locations in Trieste. This one lasted the longest.)

»*Capriccio Bar*« was just a step away from the entrance to Joyce's building. I was a bit confused when the waiter brought me my two unnamed coffees. Literally no name. My Cappuccino Odyssey was statistically compromised. I asked the waiter to tell me the brand of coffee. "No name," he replied with a big smile. "This Trieste coffee. This the best!"

No shit. Sounds like a piece from Ulysses. Cool.

The door opened and a woman came out. At first I was going to ask her who lived on the second floor, but I changed my mind. It doesn't matter.

I drank »this the best« espresso + cappuccino and walked by the building. There was a memorial plaque:

»*Ho scritto qualcosa. Il primo episodio del mio nuovo romanzo Ulisse è scritto.*«

James Joyce

16 giugno 1915

Here he wrote the first chapter of Ulysses! This is where his crazy charming odyssey began...

At the end of the building was a staircase called »*Scala James Joyce*«; very similar to the Joker Stairs in the Bronx from the movie. I jumped up some stairs like the Joker.

(That was my part in the killing joke. I didn't forget the irony.)

And there was another bar across the street. »*San Giusto*«, coffee brand: Hausbrandt. Gypsy waitress.

(Well... maybe she wasn't a Gypsy, but an Italian from the deep south of Italy... How the hell do I know? She was really kind and curious about me.)

"Ooo... americano? Qui? Ma che bello!"

(Whatever. I would never tell her about my great-grandfather. In that case, she could fall in love with me.)

- She's not a Gypsy. Since when do you even care about nationality?
- What... the fuck? Oh... it's you!
- I'm in a hurry. Let's get straight to the point.
- You in a hurry? I thought you own all the time in the world.
- I'm a beggar. I don't own anything.
- Interesting. So you're a Communist?
- No. My so-called son was. Please cut the crap. I see you admire the Jesuit?
- Who?
- Irish Jesuit. You've been watching his apartment for quite some time.
- Oh... »Jesuit«! Well... if that's the name you chose, then

yes, I have.
- I'll give you a hint. His hint actually. A quote.
- I'm listening.
- »*We are all born in the same way but we all die in different ways.*«
- New note for my wall.
- Indeed. Think about it now, without fear. And...
- And?
- Be careful with quotations.

Motherfucker vanished in an instant. And as usual he left me in doubt. No surprise. But why hurry? What for? Some Armageddon on his schedule?

I was a little pissed.

The non-Gypsy waitress brought me another portion of coffee. I wanted to think about something other than my coffee friend.

My brilliant brief history of the US encouraged me to continue with a brief history of capitalism as well.

The Italian Renaissance took place here from the fourteenth to the seventeenth century. It changed the world dramatically.

Capitalism began in northern Italy in the late Middle Ages. It changed the world dramatically.

Capitalism is unbreakable. It is neither an economic nor political system. It is a metaphysical, partly religious system that provides people with goods, things, objects, even God as an object. People know and believe that objects bring them happiness. The more things you have, the more your happiness increases. Money can even buy God. A metaphysical system with such an eschatology (and without any epistemology) cannot be destroyed.

People buy things not because they need them. They buy

things to fill the existential emptiness, the vulgarity of their existence. And in the end, people buy shopping itself, not products. They buy the ritual of shopping, so the ritual connects them more closely to the ultimate object of them all – God. It is impossible to break or fight such a strong faith.

»*The more you consume the less you live.*«
(Said a French writer full of alcohol. Alcohol was his only serious indulgence. I like that kind of metaphysics.)

Without brains, you need money. And you need God. God as a symptom. You buy God just like any other medicine. God exists, there is no doubt about it – he is part of human language. Human organ. Your stocks are safe. God is a blue chip.

The symptom reveals the cause: boredom. Human society is not dependent on economics or politics. It is based on existential boredom. Most people's lives are a combination of boredom and fear. Boredom shows the past, fear determines the future. The present is a joke.

(A killing joke, for those who understand it.)

This is why capitalism is unbreakable: it can erase boredom with shopping and reduce fear with divine protection.

(The West invented resurrection, the East invented reincarnation. Same shit, different package.)

Therefore, the basic function of capitalism is metaphysical and fully compatible with religion. Dogmata are more important than data.

To prove the metaphysical essence of capitalism, just looking at the dollar bill is enough: IN GOD WE TRUST is what really matters, not presidential portraits. The answer to the most important metaphysical question could not be simpler.

Does the American Dream exist? – NO.
Does it work? – YES.
In this context, knowledge is a burden, religion is salvation.

The Earth can be flat all around the globe again.

No one needs history. History cannot exist. People are basically conservative, frozen in time. Time is a fiction. Mistakes are made, the same ones over and over again. Fiction prevails, history is a mental disorder. Constantine the Great converted the Roman Empire into Christianity, a fictional empire, the most powerful rule of all time. His astonishing achievement was actually a conservative revolution. He understood the sublime method of crowd control as Julius Caesar never did. Constantine did not humiliate the empire, but expanded it and reached the level of a literal divine state. God became his private property.

I needed a break, so I continued walking to the seaside promenade. My steps were slow. I sat down on a bench on the »*Riva del Mandracchio*«. I felt happiness. My happiness was my responsibility, even my duty.

In the last two weeks, the pain has intensified. I had to rest more often. Opioids have done their job so far. But I could feel the difference. Like some fluid all over my body, a strange energy burning inside me.

As I sat on the bench and looked at all the buildings – Austrian buildings – along the promenade, I realized that there was something about the Austrians that I had to explain:

1. WW1 began with the assassination of Archduke Franz Ferdinand of Austria

2. WW2 was designed by a frustrated Austrian painter

3. WW3 was theoretically prepared by the Austrian economist Friedrich von Hayek

The holy trinity today – originally an Austrian idea – includes: deregulation, privatization, low taxes. A recipe for total disaster. Milton Friedman imported Hayek's ideas to Chicago and won – like Hayek before him – the Nobel Prize.

The holy trinity became the constitution of the world. Warren Buffett (!) described the process with a Marxist term: class struggle. Although I am not a Marxist, I accept the definition: WW3 is just another class struggle.

(On my personal top of the list of greatest idiocies of all time, Friedman is number one because of his portrayal of economics as a hard science; second place was won by Marx for his incredible prophecy: »*From each according to his ability, to each according to his needs.*«; third place goes to Paul the Apostle for his justification of the correct and not blasphemous haircut.)

»*The problem of our time is that the economy is globalized, but politics is not. A revolution is needed to draft new laws. People have forgotten that the revolutions of 1776 and 1789 were essentially fiscal revolts.*«

(Said a French writer with a terrible fate: he was born rich and intelligent. No wonder he solved the problem with a lot of cocaine and alcohol. This was the only solution to preserve his intelligence intact.)

<u>Any reign or government in history can choose between two options:</u>

1. Give people something to eat
2. Let people starve

<u>Results:</u>

1. Peace
2. Slaughterhouse

In the second case, people need something strong and

powerful enough to make them forget how hungry they really are. Instead of food, the only dish on the menu is hatred. Hate tastes delicious. People, hungry as motherfuckers, adore its taste.

The future of human society is totalitarian. Politicians are not corrupt. Politicians dont't lie. Politicians are waiters who serve the masses exactly what the masses want to eat. It is a mutual relationship, mutual satisfaction. The truth is never on the menu because lies taste so much better. A lie in politics is not a lie, it's a Michelin star restaurant. Politicians are as much idiots as their voters, nothing more and nothing less.

Ironic government is not possible. Humor is intelligent.

My predictable narrative stops here. I fell off the bench with terrible abdominal pain. I almost lost consciousness. Some people called an ambulance. Lying on the pavement, helpless, I understood the hint about quotations: my notes did not give me power to overcome death. I spent the next two days in the hospital. Doctors removed my appendix. My coffee friend was right: I did not fear. I knew it wasn't' the end yet. We all die in different ways. This wasn't my way. I was on the other side in the middle of the ocean: my path is already chosen there.

The surgery at the hospital was quick and easy. Routine. I went home the second day. In the meantime, I even complited my political analysis. The conclusion was simple: everything revolves around 9/11. But the point is: which 9/11? New York 2001? – Of course not. The Twins were the result, not the cause.

9/11/1973, the USA-sponsored Chilean coup d'état, was the true Rubicon of our time. The first hit of the neoliberal, metaphysical revolution. Ever since all the children are insane.

I did it. I FUCKIN' DID IT!

A few days after my appendectomy, I visited the James

Joyce Museum.

The museum was not the real motive. I just followed the »Jesuit«. He became my shadow in Trieste. My unexpected guest, my guide, my friend.

»*To love a book is, above all, to love it's author: we want to meet him again, we want to spend our days with him.*«

(Said a fearless French writer I like. Look him up, you won't regret his company.)

Bora disappeared again for a while. Silver sea, like lead. Silence screaming as usual. The threat was obvious: winter was coming. I took a look at the castle on the hill: »*Castello di San Giusto*«. I've never been there. I couldn't do it because the context was too Kafkaesque: a dying man wants to touch a phantom. Fuck the castle.

»*Caffetteria Cavana*« appeared on my way, empty, me the only guest, coffee brand Illy.

(I noticed the company logo for the first time: »Live HappILLY«. I promised I would, as far as it goes.)

Memories. Suddenly. Why? Since I came to Trieste, I have had no memories. Fear, lots of fear, yes, but no memories. Why now? My last temptation? An unpleasant surprise. People, places. Hostile ghosts. My father, never knew him, died drunk in a car crash, age twenty-seven, although not a rock star. A girlfriend, age twenty-seven, not a rock star, tried to force me to have kids. I'd rather jerk off for the rest of my life. She left, had children, loans, a dog. We met by chance a decade later. I'm tired, she said. My bosses: always surprised every time I quit. They couldn't blackmail me: I had no mortgage, no obligations to the bank.

»*If my memories overcome me, I will die.* «

(The French writer who wrote this was very intelligent and

even more courageous. Now tell me: how could I not like him?)

My whole life has been a reduction. Removal. Cutting the bullshit. No wonder, I decided to join the nation of the dead. My cancer is no surprise: I worked hard to get it.

Easy come easy go. Memories. A worthless possibility of consciousness. You do not fight memories. Not even ignore them. You smile without saying a word. Silence erases them. You don't remember something that doesn't exist. You don't let the memories kill you. You despise the past. Now you live. Now you can die. You sold your soul: it was a fair deal. You owe nothing to anyone.

The museum was as sarcastic as Joyce: it consisted of only one room. Like an unexpected story, just like Ulysses. Another killing joke.

Joyce first arrived in Trieste in October 1904 and left for the last time in July 1920, completely disappointed with the new Italian administration after WW1. Maybe that's why the Italians sacrificed nothing more than a single room in honor of some crazy Irish bastard that nobody reads.

The only useful information I found in the so-called museum was the name of the brothel »*Il Metro Cubo*« in the red light district of Trieste from the beginning of the twentieth century. Between the Jewish ghetto and the seaside quarter, there were more than forty brothels in the old town at that time. I can imagine that Joyce took a tremendous opportunity when he wrote his crazy fifteenth episode of Ulysses – Circe – set in a brothel.

I found some narrow streets there. No people, no cafés, no story. Joyce's shadow led me away, I obeyed the instructions.

Use your feet, motherfucker, while you can still walk! My daily dose of opioids increased. In addition, I was given some extra analgesics after leaving the hospital.

(Although I didn't feel any pain in my stomach. The scar on my belly was almost invisible. I will die without formal aesthetic damage. Cancer will eat me up and destroy me from the inside out. My skin will turn yellow and yellow eyes will look at me from the other side.)

After a long walk I reached a gas station on the hill. Trucks, dirt, garbage, stink – American type of environment. Port everywhere. Huge rusty oil tanks, out of order. Steelworks in ruins. Blade Runner scenery.

(»*Time to die*« says Roy, the replicant in the movie, and smiles. Smiles and dies. He knew. He knew the trick exactly. And he accepted it. He admitted defeat. This is why he was really more human than humans.)

A few trucks in the parking lot, fast food »*Eni Café*«, Lavazza coffee. Staring at the sea for an hour, I gathered enough energy to return back home. I was late, shadows rising from the darkness were all around me. Unknown shadows, taking care of me. My night watch in the forest, protecting me from the beasts.

On the bridge, next to the Joyce statue, I took my first shot of morphine with a needle. Not from pain, but from exhaustion. Good night, I said to all the shadows, to Joyce, to Canal Grande. I was grateful.

The night on the balcony was cold. There were ten inches of snow in New York, I read the news in the Times. There is no snow in Trieste; if there rarely is, it melts during the day. Death no longer scared me, but the snow could be a serious obstacle. I needed clean streets to keep walking. I was losing my strength and weight too obviously. I slept longer. Many people say that it's a blessing to die in your sleep. Not to know you're gone. Not feeling pain.

I despise such an attitude from the bottom of my heart. The fear of death simply disgusts me. I disgusted myself for it.

Both of my political analyzes included fear as well. The West invented resurrection, the East invented reincarnation. Two different methods with the same goal: to ignore death. Deny death. All political actions arise out of fear. Therefore, death is pure politics.

Technology is another tool, another attempt to even defeat death. Multiply yourself! Buy yourself a clone! But we fail again. Death is the only truth. There are no alternatives. Our only choice is to admit defeat.

Jesus died on the cross, he really died just to show us the truth, not the resurrection. Honesty made him divine and dead. We cannot accuse him of hypocrisy, but only desperation. It is no coincidence that he often repeated the phrase: »*Whoever has ears, let them hear.*«

(His so-called father didn't hear the call. He took a permanent vacation.)

The second shot of morphine made me feel a warm tranquility.

»Drug addiction« is an oxymoron. »Addiction« is a misnomer in the phrase. Drugs, pills, alcohol, all kinds of substances – most people use them. To struggle against pain. To deal with invisible, abstract pain. Reality – whatever that means – is the problem. There is something terribly wrong with reality if no one can stand it.

(Those who can are liars or lobotomy convalescents.)

Normality consists of fear and pain. If reality is normal, you have to be insane not to take drugs.

I sat stoned on the balcony for like an hour before I went to sleep. »*The universe needs more good editors, God knows*« Kurt Vonnegut said. I had to remember this and tell it to my coffee friend.

(I knew he won't give a fuck. But he'll be laughing like crazy and that's what counts.)

## THE VELVET UNDERGROUND: VENUS IN FURS

It's been a while. And it's fucking cold now. Bora rules without mercy, very often with speeds close to 100 mph, sometimes even 130 mph.

Hard to smoke outside. Now I take coffee with me, I hide somewhere in narrow streets, secret empty corners, even tunnels. At home, I learned how to make coffee in the »Moka Pot«. Just black, I keep it in a bottle on the go.

I still walk every day. I don't panic, I'm just enjoying my steps. I'm trying to finish my soundtrack, select tunes, thousands of them. I narrowed down the selection: American musicians only. An elegant solution, although not entirely satisfactory.

(Completing the soundtrack was an impossible task, no doubt about it. But that's exactly my point: I will fail, of course. I admitted defeat a long time ago. I announce my defeat without any regret or embarrassment. It's hard to admit defeat, especially for an American. We were raised to win. Defeat ain't American. It is a disgrace forbidden in the land of the free, where no one is brave enough to lose. I realized, on the contrary, my defeat is all I have. All I ever had. And all I have to lose. I will try to be – at least – a beautiful loser. I will try to lose with style.)

I should stick more to rock'n'roll. Even all my political analyzes could easily be solved and replaced with one single motto: SEX & DRUGS & ROCK'N'ROLL. The most powerful logo of all time. It scared the shit out of America like neither the Communists nor the Gooks had ever done before.

(Don't get me wrong: I'm not advertising some profane hedonistic attitude. I'm talking about the danger. A serious danger that changed the world. The Pentagon was capable of setting the jungle on fire, but powerless against rock'n'roll.)

I take morphine occasionally. Not to confront my pain, but to keep my steps steady and safe. And feeling good. Obviously I'm going to die a drug addict, which I've never been in my life. But not like all those pathetic junkies on New York streets: disgusting, filthy monuments of human misery.

I declare drug addiction to be my radical political statement.

Unfortunately, I will never start a political party. If realised, it should be global. Remember the French writer's advice? – Active desertion. Sober people are bored and boring. No wonder they build concentration camps to have at least a little fun in their lives. My appeal would be: get high! Not like some pathetic hippies, those imbeciles didn't understand anything. Get high with attitude!

Get high, dress nicely, read, walk! Never consume weed! It will make you passive and useless. Take hard drugs, risk overdose, invite death, be dignified, clean, elegant. Intelligence is your weapon. Respect obsessive compulsive order and always put things where they fucking belong. Get stoned and responsible: the higher you get, the less mistakes you make. Stand still or sit down quietly if you take too much – you never know, it might be OD,  so don't make a fuss because it's pointless: you fucked up totally, congratulations! Be aware of what you are doing: your resistance.

Never use violence, burn the fucking Bible – it only

worships violence. Fuck the Holy Trinity, fuck Allah, fuck Buddha, fuck Jehovah, fuck Confucius, fuck the American president, fuck the drunken Russian tsar, fuck the Pope!

Take a shot and smile.

Junkies of the world, unite!

(If anyone is able to implement my idea, please use the copyright free of charge as my legacy.)

I will most likely still be forty-nine when I die.

Let there not be no misunderstanding: there is no difference between nineteen and forty-nine. I've known this since I was a teenager. My lack of self-confidence forced me to be my own censor: I thought I was naive or stupid. I thought I had to wait. Grow up, whatever that means. I thought my knowledge was poor. I thought I was in for a secret. An explanation will appear later.

Now I know I wasn't wrong. Only my private censorship was naive. In fact, I saw clearly, my perspective was accurate. I saw death. It wasn't a mistake, just a horror that the young man had a hard time accepting.

So I have bad news for you: age doesn't matter. You will feel the same at nineteen, forty-nine or ninety-nine years old. The same fear, the same passion, the same hope. And the only difference? – Your fear will increase as much as you get older.

But you have kids, your blood, your future? – These precious gems will gladly bury you not just once, but three times if necessary – if you leave them enough money.

Last but not least, your body will betray you, and you won't find any additional wisdom about it.

Are you scared shitless now? – You should be.

Only fear and defeat await you out there. Vegetables instead of meat, so-called healthy living habbits, bad breath, hairy body, back-to-nature-bullshit, bad sex, no sex (who really wants to have sex with you anyway), visiting infantile shrinks or hypocritical church service on Sunday won't help you. You lose, motherfucker!

I have the right to think as I do now. I traveled across the ocean for this. I don't feel rage, I feel release.

Joyce's shadow, among others, follows me wherever I go. He left his homeland early in his life, I did it at the end of mine. He hated Ireland, I don't hate America. »*In the particular is contained the universal*« he said – this is how he could live in Trieste and write about Dublin at the same time.

I bought a warm coat and a blanket so I could walk and hide and sit and drink my coffee safe from Bora.

I take long walks, I even reached the state border. To be precise: Trieste is already the Italian border in the very northeast of Italy. But I'm talking literally about the border crossing: the highway, light traffic, a few grocery stores, even a casino. No police, just peace. Nothing like El Paso. To my right the Slavic world from my standing point across Eastern Europe, Russia, Siberia to Vladivostok on Pacific coast. To my left the beginning of the Latin world, which ends at Cape Horn in South America. An impressive perspective.

One night in a bar I was talking to a group of Italians – friends of my gay-cocaine-supply-bartender – about this border. They actually talked to me after the bartender introduced me as an American. I was silent. Their trick was easy to unravel: they were all Italian nationalists, apparently feeling it their duty to teach me the only sacred truth about historical facts, as they called their dogmatic interpretation. Trieste ain't just the border between the (primitive) Slavic and (noble) Latin world, it is also the first point on the line of the much more important Trieste –

Vienna – Gdansk border, which bisects Europe: the left side represents civilization, the right side of the border the territory of savages.

(Hitler's theory was quite similar to this one. Eternal European nationalist bullshit. My great-grandfather would be delighted to confirm that. I drank my tonic water without commenting on the topic and left. I never took cocaine from a fascist gay fucker again.)

Bora drove everyone off the streets. I could lean back into the wind and still stand upright. Escape was urgent, I chose a tunnel without a pedestrian zone, no cars intrusion, empty.

I saw two chairs. You don't usually see chairs in the middle of tunnels. The light was dim, but I recognized the shadow sitting on one of them.

The other chair was there empty, waiting for me.

- Good evening! Come on, you're going to freeze out there!
- Is it? Already? The evening?
- Almost. Did you take your blanket?
- I did. Good evening to you too! I see, you brought us chairs.
- Nice, isn't it?
- Nice to see you again, I must say.
- Indeed. Unfortunately, this is our last meeting. I just wanted to say goodbye to you before I leave.
- You're leaving? A lot of work? Judgment Day, Armaggedeon, another Great Flood plans?
- Spare me such crap please! I'm leaving because you don't need me any
- more.
- You sure? You trust me that much?

- I'm sure. And besides – it's not a matter of trust, as you know.
- I know. Can I ask you one last question?
- Only if it's the right one. People always expect answers. But in fact...
- ... questions are important, not answers. Stupid questions give us idiotic answers.
- You are a good student. So ask, please!
- Did you create irony on purpose? Joke's on you, because you're powerless too?
- No, no, no – you're completely wrong! I do control everything! But the truth is much worse than you ever imagined: this-all-there-is is... just as good as it gets. Fuck it...
- Huh! Wel... then... yeah... fuck it!
- I hope you are not disappointed?
- Of course not. Anyway – I was waiting for you for another reason.
- Oh... and what would that be?
- I wanna tell you a joke.
- A joke?
- If you don't mind?
- I'm all ears! Better be a good one!
- Actually it's a riddle. And it ain't mine. I stole it from...
- Whatever. Go on!
- OK. It goes like this:

The cock crew
The sky was blue:
The bells in heaven
Were striking eleven.
Tis time for this poor soul
To go to heaven.

- Nice. What is it?
- You don't know the answer?
- Of course not! I have no fuckin' idea. Tell me!
- It's the fox burying his grandmother under a hollybush.
- NO SHIT! Now you're the one kidding me!
- Do you like it?
- Absolutely! You surprised me. I'm proud of you, honestly. It's just that...
- It's formally a riddle?
- No, no, not at all! It's just... it doesn't sound French at all.
- It isn't. Why should it be?
- You quote those French fuckers so often. But that... just ain't French. This is the product of some otherwise sophisticated sick mind. So tell me: who wrote this?
- The guy from the bridge.
- From the bridge? You mean like the bridge here in Trieste?
- Yeap. Bridge over the Canal Grande.
- Oh! That guy! The Jesuit! Again.
- I believe he would disagree with your characterization.
- Not a chance, trust me! I knew the guy.
- You did? Of course you did...
- I remember him quite well. He had a remarkable sense of irony. No wonder it's his joke! Pardon me – a riddle.
- So you two were talking? Like us?
- No. Never. He wouldn't speak to me, he was too proud for that. But he sent me some questions. In writing, of course. A true gentleman, indeed.
- Some questions? Like what?
- Like for example: is baptism with a mineral water

116

valid? Can you imagine? I almost pissed my pants laughing. What a spirit!
- Sweet Jesus...
- About him too, yes!
- No doubt, no doubt...
- He even had the guts to go public with his mineral water question. In those days... it was a dangerous act, believe me!
- Yes, it was. And it still is.
- You're exaggerating a bit. Anyway, forget about mineral water. You two have something in common, you know?
- I never thought of that.
- You were both frantically searching for words. One word even. The last one. »*My kingdom for a horse!*«
- Maybe... in some past tense.
- Don't be offended.
- I'm not. There is no kingdom, simple as that.
- Correct. And the horse is dead. He, the Jesuit, knew it, just as you do now.
- And?
- From time to time the two of you suspected what if it was just the opposite, what if it is the...
- ... silence. Bullshit. Silence means nothing. Silence is beautiful and meaningless.
- And brave.
- And brave, yes.
- Fine. I'm done with you, my dear friend.
- You are?
- I am. I just have to remind you about the mask.
- The Death mask, of course... My personal Venetian Catch 22.

- Catch 22! An American solution, not a French one. How appropriate!
- If you say so.
- I do. Anything else you want to say?
- A farewell word?
- If you want to.
- As a matter of fact... yes... I'd like to borrow your so-called son's advise.
- Surprise... Okay, do it!
- »*Therefore do not worry about tomorrow, for tomorrow will worry about itself...*
- »*Each day has enough trouble of its own.*« He had some good moments, I give him that ...
- Thank you and... goodbye!
- God bless you!

I was sitting in the tunnel. Alone. I was alone most of my life. Girlfriends yes, but no marriage, no kids. A dog, once. My loneliness was not a punishment. I worked hard to enjoy it. I deserved it. Being alone was the greatest reward I ever received. I was rewarded with time. Time to observe, time to feel grace, time to read, time to think, time to make love slowly, very slowly. Time to prepare. Time to meet death.

Darkness in the tunnel, darkness outside as I was returning home. An unexpected thought occurred to me: would it somehow be possible for me to NOT leave my body behind? I was thrilled. How could this be done? Suicide was out of the question. Maybe I found a new task, the last one.

(At home, I first checked the mineral water problem. It was true: the Jesuit did question the validity of soda-baptism.)

Given the fact that there is no last word, I decided to formulate some final questions. These are examples:

1. Why can't women learn how to clean shoes properly?
2. Why did men invent patriarchy instead of simply learning to effectively control premature ejaculation?
3. How is it possible that a bat does not shit on its head while sleeping?

I won't even try to find answers. Now I have to fail better. This is my try:

»*Even in our deepest, most lasting friendships, we never speak so openly as when we face a blank page and address an unknown reader.*«

(Said a French... oh, fuck that!)

BONUS TRACK: SWANS: LEAVING MEANING

I am leaving meaning now. I sold my soul. The Master is waiting for me.

IN GIRUM IMUS NOCTE ET CONSUMIMUR IGNI